Today, I choose to be Happy

"Get to know your inner self
and start building a happy life."

Luz Pino

Published by Ibukku
www.ibukku.com
Graphic design: Índigo Estudio Gráfico
Cover photo: Makoto Seimori en Pixabay
Copyright © 2020 Luz Pino
ichoosetobehappy2020@gmail.com
ISBN Paperback: 978-1-64086-756-7
ISBN eBook: 978-1-64086-757-4

ÍNDICE

Through humility, I want to express my thoughts through this book. It is the first one I have written and I feel as though it is part of my life's purpose to help other people grow spiritually and encourage them to move towards their dreams. I am thankful to God and to the universal laws that allowed me to make a positive contribution to everyone who reads this book.

I, myself, continue to discover virtues and talents that motivate me to grow and be a better version of myself...

But I dare to promote change and the discovery of your inner self, because that is where you will find all the answers.

"Finding my happiness... walking in a constant awakening."

Luz A. Pino

Thank you, my husband, for your effort and dedication, thank you for all you did to help me make this dream a reality...

Thank you for your valuable contributions and for believing that we could make it...

Once again we did it and we did it together...

"Because as far as our mind can reach, that's as far as we'll go."

All of our lives together!

I love you...

PROLOGUE

This book aims to provide ideas that are useful in motivating the reader's journey to his or her inner world. That unexplored world that has immense undiscovered riches for every person. An inner world so vast that it holds everything a person requires to live a successful and happy life. None of this is a secret; it is within the reach of everyone who wants to fully benefit from this earth and who truly longs to be happy. Even though the word **happy**, may have many connotations, in the end happiness is only a state of tranquility that motivates and drives us to live fully.

It is a positive concept of life in all its forms. To achieve true happiness is to reach the place where we can live peacefully in spite of the difficult moments and ups and downs to which all human beings are exposed to on a daily basis. I would be lying if I said that happiness is reached when all the suffering or difficulties are over, but let us be aware that life is made up of good and unpleasant moments, with the latter being where we become truly strong. So we need to learn to be happy with our life and its circumstances. I am convinced that as we delve into the content of this book, we will be able to acquire new ways of thinking and behaving, enabling us to experience different results and an improved quality of life.

This book is suitable for all kinds of people. It contains concepts for personal development and improving interpersonal relationships. If you read it and put some of the ideas presented here into practice, you will perceive notable and important changes within yourself and your environment.

ACKNOWLEDGMENTS

To my husband Carlos who has been my partner, my great support, my unconditional friend and my strength. A beautiful rainbow that puts the most beautiful colors in my days; the man I respect, admire and love deeply. For my mother Asseneth who brought the fundamental principles of life to me; whom I love and admire for her effort and dedication. For my father Juan who, although not physically present anymore, is in my heart and I continue to love him. For my beloved sister Victoria, admirable woman of strength, courage and love. To my brother Helmer, an inspiring and respectable being who leaves traces of blessing wherever he goes. To my nieces and nephews Luisa, Santiago, Juan Jacobo, Emmanuel, Laura Sofia and Dulce Maria; who have filled my life with blessings, joy and love. To Dr. Carlos E. Cuero, from whom I acquired very pertinent knowledge for my life. To John Jairo Soto, who has taught me through his wisdom and whom I admire for his valuable contributions to the lives of so many people. To my friends and all the people who have passed through my life, who in one way or another have brought great blessings and from which I have learned to grow and evolve.

Special acknowledgment to Dr. Elizabeth C.W Jones for her dedication and support while on proofreading for English translation.

INTRODUCTION

Who hasn't dreamed of being happy, succeeding and achieving their dreams? Who hasn't daydreamed of those places and times so longed for, but when awoken , they realize those are just thoughts that crossed their minds and vanished in an instant as fast as they came?

Many of us have felt the frustration of watching the days, months and perhaps years go by feeling that we have not reached our goals; with the bitter taste of what could have been and was not. With the nostalgia of not having given our best, of not having risked doing something we wanted to do, or simply with the inability to face a hermetic and increasingly materialistic system that tries to limit and firmly point out everything beyond its parameters.

Regardless of your age, in this book you will have the opportunity to discover different ways of seeing life and to understand that we are unlimited beings who can learn to give our best and receive the best that life has to offer; how to get better results in everything you undertake. You will know that you can be part of the change, that nothing happens by chance; that everything has a purpose, because even the adverse moments bring great teachings and make us get all the strength and courage that we never thought we had inside.

Any age is suitable to care for one's happiness. The best time to feel fulfilled and live a life of purpose is now.

Human beings are formed in a womb by the union of two lives. We had a time of gestation and then we were given birth. It was there that we manifested our first strengths and without knowing it, fought our first battle at the time of birth. This is the encounter with the outside world and everything around us is new, impressive and wonderful. Seeing mom and dad for the first time, maybe also our brothers and friends, the doctors and nurses, who give us a special welcome. Our adventure outside the womb begins. We begin to live according to the teachings of each family; we are given the knowledge with which we will live from that moment on. Like a sponge we absorb every word, every gesture, every behavior from our environment. We learn the way we will treat others and how we believe we will be treated. We are instilled with self-determination or fear and a way of doing things. If we are lucky we are taught values and discipline,a love of work, nature and life. We learn that there are times to talk and times to listen. It is the principles fostered at home that will definitely make us, the reflection of our parents. These fundamentals will be the foundation on which our life will be built, which will later be externalized through our actions.

Parents are our first teachers, our heroes and our refuge. They are the ones who provide us with security, who correct us, motivate us and make our lives happy. In them we find a model to follow and with their help we face the first obstacles.

A new stage begins in which for the first time we separate from our parents to start being independent; it is the school phase where different people begin to arrive, bringing new things to our existence. There are the teachers who will be our guides and through whom we will learn, according to what they have to teach us; both in knowledge and in values. It is there where we practically initiate new relationships with other people and make ourselves known to a completely strange world; each one with a different essence. Those who will occupy important places in our hearts arrive, as well as those with whom we will live undesirable moments. Each day is a constant growth in knowledge and stature. We are developing our capacities and showing the potential that each one of us has. Situations begin to arise that allow us to assume responsibilities and acquire rights that little by little give us, in one way or another, a direction for our lives. It is there in that growth, both physical and emotional, where our first challenges arise; either in the academic part or in our personal life. They initiate changes in our body and in our way of being. Our first strong emotional experiences occur. We cannot ignore the fact that childhood and adolescence have their own difficulties, creating fears and affecting our emotions. In the adolescent stage, we experience very strong emotions, because we have responsibilities, but also a number of dreams and goals to achieve or often the opposite; we do not even know what direction to take in our life. Regardless of all of this, we wake up every morning ready to live a new day without thinking about what will happen next, but there is in our heart a longing to do something else; unreasonable and daring ideas arise to undertake a journey, a business, to give our life a complete makeover and many times, they remain just that, ideas without action. By the time we realize this, we are adults and that is when we stop to analyze the state of our lives, coming to the conclusion that we are stuck. It seems that we find ourselves going around in the same place. As much as we yearn and strive to change things, everything remains the same.

We see other people succeeding, reaching their goals, and we ask ourselves: Why can't I get everything I've dreamed of?

That's when many people make wrong decisions and in the midst of that desperation to find what they think will bring them happiness, they commit misguided acts guided by emotion and anxiety. Some get involved in improper business, others get involved with a partner hoping to find some financial stability, others may lose their dignity or go beyond the dignity of others in order to achieve their goals, but many times the price paid for achieving goals like this is not taken into account. Usually we look for happiness in something external, we think it is a destiny or something we do not deserve. Other people may think that happiness will come when they have a lot of money, recognition, or when they find the partner of their dreams. These might be some of the models of happiness sold to us, but we don't realize that what we have been looking for outside, for so long, is inside each of us. There, in that corner of ourselves that has always been waiting to be discovered.

CHAPTER ONE
"Getting to know myself"

Most human beings watch on automatic. We are used to looking at something and easily make an opinion on the first thing that comes to mind, according to our own perception. We become experts at expressing concepts about the lives of others. We easily detect their mistakes and even dare to judge them. The capacity we acquire to question from the ego, the way others think, speak and act, is incredible. We have become eminent judges who even make judgments on their lives, since many times our questioning does not end up only in our minds, but we take it to meetings where the topic of discussion is other people. Getting to the point of generating negative feelings and resentments.

It is so normal to criticize others, but so bitter to know that they are criticizing us. We can't stand being the center of some conversation where they give their opinion about our life. This is so uncomfortable, isn't it?

It would be better to focus on getting to know ourselves. Keeping in mind that, if I know myself as an individual, I can learn to have control over my thoughts, emotions and attitudes; thus allowing me to get better results.

Part of knowing ourselves is being aware that life is Being and Being is composed of Spirit, Soul and Body. In this chapter we will stop to learn about the soul, which is where emotions come from. The term "emotion" has its origin in the Latin word *emotio*, which means movement or impulse.

An emotion can generate an immediate biological reaction that is expressed through facial gestures, tone of voice, nervous system activity, and heartbeat, among others.

Emotions establish my position in relation to my environment and include responses such as aggression, laughter, or tears , depending on the type of emotion being experienced. Emotions are impulses in our thinking that lead us to act in certain ways in different circumstances. We may not be aware of them and they may bring about favorable or unfavorable consequences. Emotions lead us to acquire momentary behaviors, which powerfully mark our life.

And where do emotions come from?

Emotions arise from a thought. This can be positive or negative. The thought produces a sensation in us that brings a reaction. It depends on how we are thinking at the time and how much self-control we have in any given situation. It is very valuable to know that each human being has the capacity to control his emotions and not let them dominate him. To reach this point we must begin by knowing ourselves.

Being sensible when speaking or acting raises us to a higher level that allows us to live in harmony with our surroundings. We become generators of peace.

At the beginning of this chapter we observed the ease we have in seeing and analyzing the lives of others, and this is one of the most deeply rooted and common obstacles that prevent us from advancing towards self-awareness.

"Now, I will no longer look outward, but will look inward. Where my weaknesses and my strengths are."

Within me is the fear that keeps me from doing different things, the resentment, the hatred, the bitterness, the lack of faith, the insecurity; there is the criticism that is only a way of hiding all that I have not been able to achieve. The most gratifying thing is to know that within me there is also strength, potential, talent, the ability to project my ideas and undertake them, love, forgiveness, confidence in myself and in others.

Within me is the power to change and master emotions. If a negative thought is generated in my mind, I myself have the ability to identify it and decide whether to give it strength or to replace it with one that brings benefit to my life. When I think well, I definitely act well; more so if I think driven by negative impulses, I will most certainly have a negative reaction and the result will be equally negative.

Thoughts are the source of life. From a thought the most prodigious projects arise. A fact is born from a thought, and the thought is fed with all the information available to our senses, this information enters and lodges directly in our subconscious. Our eyes and ears are the filter of what reaches our brain; through them passes all the information and for this reason we must take care of what we see and hear, since our life is filled with it. According to the nature of the thought, so will be the results that will be manifested.

Let us be aware of what is good for us, what motivates us and helps us to grow as people.

Being aware of my mistakes and my successes, makes me strong in my weakness because I learn to have control over those weak areas and I can know what the right attitude is in front of any circumstance that life presents to me.

If I understand that I don't look at others to judge or criticize, but look at myself, to know myself and have mastery of my character, I will realize that within me is the strength, the capacity and everything I need to achieve my goals and then I will have already overcome a great personal challenge. Change begins with me; I will not seek to change the world, but only to change myself. Definitely, "if I change, my whole environment changes." Starting with small actions is how you achieve great transformations.

One point that is decisive to begin to know myself is to learn to free myself from the old concepts of good and bad; understanding that there is no absolute truth about things, that there is no last word. What is good for me may be bad for someone else, or vice versa. Examples of this are the cultures, the customs of each country; what in one place can be done with total freedom, in another can be a punishable offence. For that reason, let us be aware of the damage we cause to ourselves and to others when we speak ill of another person. Words have a lot of power. Let's use that power to positively impact others, to provide a word of encouragement, to bless and generate well-being.

Words are also powerful on the negative end and to destroy. Every negative word that I utter either about myself or another person is a destroying curse that attracts unfavorable vibrations. A word can hurt deeply or it can heal and bring joy.

If we take time to internalize, we can discover the true meaning of life, that purpose which gives our existence a special and different value.

On this path of getting to know ourselves better, we also learn to love ourselves and become confident people, and this generates that we begin to enjoy more of those moments of solitude that allow us to instruct ourselves and move forward in discovering those inner treasures that we didn't know were there. You simply learn to enjoy solitude and that is when you will begin to experience that your life has the same meaning, either alone or in the company of someone else.

The person who is sure of themselves enjoys their moments of solitude just as much as when they are in the company of others.

Within each person there is a winner. For example, an athlete runs his own race, his achievements are personal, and thus teamwork and triumphs are achieved for the whole group; everyone has to run his own race.

You too can discover the winner in you, you just have to be brave and determined. Know your weaknesses and become strong in them. Discover your strengths and make them even more powerful. Being a winner requires attitude and discipline. If you take the time to get to know yourself and discover your mistakes, not to feel guilty but to identify those areas that have not allowed you to move forward, you will reach a level of fulfillment that only winners can enjoy.

Anything is possible, you just need to believe in yourself. Believe that you are a special being. Believing that from your mother's womb, you're already a champion. That if you're reading this book today, it is because you're not one more, it is because there is a purpose for you and you are making the decision to be better than yesterday.

Knowing who you are makes you powerful. A human being's greatest challenge is to master himself. The man who manages to master his emotions and learns to have the right attitude to any circumstance is destined to be happy, to succeed in whatever he undertakes and to enjoy privileges that seemed impossible before.

Those who allow themselves to be dominated by their emotions experience afflictions based on the guilt of others. Those who do not recognize their mistakes will never be able to know themselves and will not know what to do in the midst of uncertainty. Meanwhile, those who accept their faults, recognize them and seek change, will go through a constant transformation that will allow them to achieve greater and greater objectives for the benefit of themselves and their community. They will experience that every time they set a goal and achieve it, they broaden their vision for a bigger one and if they look back, they will only see what they have overcome.

Dare to know yourself, look at yourself in the mirror, face yourself and accept yourself as you are. And if you are going to focus on your defects, don't make excuses for them and fail to out your projects, but find the thousand ways that exist to correct them. Learn to laugh at yourself to gain confidence. Look at all your strong points and strengthen them. Give thanks for every part of your body, accept yourself and you will be accepted. Love yourself and you will be loved.

A strategy I can use as a tool to know myself, is when I see the mistakes in others, I immediately look inside myself, become aware and analyze myself. If I make the same mistake I see in someone else, I can make the decision to correct it and improve on it. I don't judge or point things out, I just reflect and thank myself for being able to see it through others and for having the ability to correct it in myself.

In this way I am part of the change and not only do I grow as a person, but with my change I transform my environment. If I used to make a mistake and I don't do it anymore, the people around me will be positively impacted and we can be part of a different society that offers a better quality of life, starting from my home and my family.

Society is made up of families; that is where change begins and each of us is part of those families. Therefore, it is within me where this transformation begins, where I find the will power and everything I need to achieve my purposes.

It is from within me that good or bad comes. Everything that contaminates a person springs from its own heart, its way of thinking and its way of perceiving life. The heart feeds on what we let into it. If I learn to analyze myself, I am also learning to select the kind of information with which I fill my mind.

What do I see? What do I hear? What kind of contribution does this or that make to my life that I am devoting my valuable time to? Am I managing my time well or am I wasting it?

To know myself is to know everything about myself; it is to discover which things I like and which things bother me, what gives me peace of mind, what prevents me from flying high, what limits me or what does not even allow me to dream. Knowing myself enables me to find out which of the circumstances I experienced in my childhood prevent me from being a winner today. It also leads me to analyze which of the wrong teachings, perhaps involuntarily on my parents' behalf, have not allowed me to know who I am, to have my own identity, to make wise decisions, to act with certainty, to launch into big projects, to be excellent at something I like to do or would have liked to be. Knowing myself reveals to me the truth of knowing that my habitual way of thinking creates the reality in which I live every day.

What is the reason why we don't know each other?

Perhaps we have been too busy doing what everyone else does without conscience; we have let ourselves be dragged into the system. Because of that counterproductive way in which we base our lives today, for example, on physical appearance, looking good in front of others, making easy money, living certain moments without measuring the consequences that could negatively affect our future. When we least think about it, we are immersed in circumstances from which we do not know how to get out, and many lose their lives in the attempt. As the phrase goes: *"What I focus on, expands."*

Without going too far, let's think about the so-called diseases of this time, such as stress and depression, and we hear about many more, not to mention suicides in both young people and adults. All these situations come from the soul. These illnesses arise from suffering caused by negative emotions and accumulation of difficult moments, sadness, defeats, loss of loved ones, complicated economic situations, and so on. But if we knew who we really are, all the strength and capacity we possess to face each of the circumstances that arise in our lives however complex they may seem, we would not have to suffer from these types of diseases that only make the situation worse; further blurring our vision.

It is my responsibility to dedicate the necessary time to getting to know who I am, to investigate my weaknesses and to work on transforming them into possibilities of renewal. To discover my strengths in order to take care of them and empower them; and if I finally decide to learn to master my emotions, then I will be taking a first big step towards happiness.

Knowing yourself will definitely result in recovering your identity, knowing who you are, where you come from and where you are going; it will allow you to be a man or woman with sound character.

Your character defines the kind of person you are.

CHAPTER TWO
"Weaknesses and Strengths"

All human beings have weaknesses and strengths. Each person is completely different from the other. Everyone has something that identifies them from each other physically and in their nature, they will never be the same. Hence the importance of not pretending that others think or behave the same way I do. Why are several children born to the same father and mother, but are different despite having the same teaching, seeing and hearing the same things?

Even twin brothers formed in the same womb are different. Each one shows a different personality. Every human being is born with a distinct character and identity. It should be the job of parents to understand their child from birth. Not only to look at them, but to observe and analyze them, since they themselves will show their weaknesses and strengths. Their likes, their temperament and their character. Hence the importance for parents to observe and accompany their children at every stage of growth and provide them with the help they need to learn to manage their weaknesses and enhance their strengths. The child shows their preferences and their potential from a very early age, but sometimes the parents do not know it and begin to change the essence of the child; laying down the information that they have in their own brain. That is, the way they think, speak and act according to the teaching they in turn received from their family, generation after generation.

I want to make a parenthesis to explain why I say that parents change the essence of the child due to lack of knowledge: It is because every human being comes to the earthly plane equipped with a clean and healthy consciousness, but at birth it is surrounded by an environment. Which one? It depends on the way each family has based its teaching and training. From birth, each person follows a kind of pattern that directs its life and turns it into an endless chain of information. For example, when parents compare their child to another child, they are inducing him/her to change his/her identity. It's as if they're pushing their child to hide behind a personality that doesn't belong to them, just to please their parents. In addition, it is as if the child is taught to lie to himself and therefore to others. The child will try to be the person his parents want to see, but not who he really is in essence. The child may lose his transparency and simply adopt the habits he sees as examples in his environment.

Let's take another example: a father who is used to drinking or smoking in front of his child, but says, "You're not going to do it". What the child really learned is that this is the way to act, not what the parent told the child not to do. We learn much more readily by example.

I am by no means accusing parents, since there are also parents who provide very good formation to their children, but it is important that we know and learn to assume that we have weaknesses and that we make mistakes; which we must recognize and know where they come from in order to correct them.

We also have strengths that we must identify in order to make the best use of them, using them for our benefit and that of our community.

From the womb, the child receives information from its parents, more directly from its mother. Their attitude, their words, their emotions, their state of mind, everything is perceived by the fetus in gestation and when the child is born, it continues to receive all the information it perceives from its environment.

It is common to see that many people have children, but they can't keep an eye on them (everyone has their own reasons), so they resort to putting the care of their children in the hands of a third person; be it a grandmother, an aunt, a nanny or someone else. In some cases, the father did not assume his role responsibly and the mother assumes the full obligation and must go out to work to meet the needs of her household. In other cases the father went elsewhere in search of economic stability; whatever the situation, what is worth noting here is that it is in the hands of whoever is in charge of educating your child to make him/her a person with an identity, prepared for life in society and capable of achieving his/her dreams.

Preparing children for life depends on this chain of information passing from person to person. In this specific case, between the children and the people around them. This is a warning for parents about the responsibility they must have at the time of begetting children and the awareness of knowing how to educate them to live a fuller life in all areas; adopting a personality that allows them to be and express themselves freely, preserving their pure essence. The sum of these foundations plays a determining role in the integrity of each person.

When a parent teaches his/her child, he/she is passing on everything he/she learned from his/her parents and surroundings. There are many circumstances that affect the fact that nowadays children do not receive from their parents the adequate training to safely assume their role in a society with forgotten principles. We must be well prepared not to succumb to the number of entities imposed by the system in order to be accepted by it, even if the price to be paid is too high. That's why people easily bow to fashions and styles that are driven only by what they see in the masses, which is why they spread the media that manipulate the mind, thus achieving that many of them depend on that consumerism that creates more and more men and women with a low self-esteem; because they dispose their mind and their senses to fill them with information that at the moment of truth, do not contribute anything positive to improve their quality of life and that little by little are clouding creativity.

Human beings are like a fountain from which clean water or dirty water can flow, it all depends on what has entered it at some point. Are we aware of what we are opening the door to our interior to? Have we stopped to think about what kind of information reaching our brain and therefore our life?

We should be responsible for what we see and hear. Let us observe the environment in which we move. Our weaknesses come from somewhere. It is our primary task to identify them and, once done, find ways to master those weaknesses.

Let us keep in mind that weaknesses are those mental paradigms that prevent us from achieving our heart's desires.

Let's look at it from this perspective, if one of my weaknesses is the fear of risking the unknown, that fear blocks me from doing things that I would like to see realized in my life. The first step is to recognize that I have been fearful and then to analyze where that fear comes from that prevents me from making a determined decision.

Let's remember that since childhood we began to acquire these weaknesses, but whatever the reason why this seed of weakness was planted, we should not look for guilt, because it has been a chain of information that must be broken by the person who has become aware. Knowing the cause of our limitations, the next step is to face it with courage.

When a person has been fearful, but decides to face that fear and succeeds in overcoming it, they feel fulfilled. Their soul is flooded in a sea of satisfaction and joy. They feel powerful and every time they achieve a goal, they feel that they can launch themselves into a greater challenge.

If I know myself, I can see within me those weaknesses that do not allow me to emerge in the way I would really like to; I can also overcome all those obstacles that I never thought I would be able to overcome. I can see what keeps me from being a winner and performing with excellence in everything I undertake.

Weaknesses create frustration. They keep us stuck thinking about what we would achieve if we were in this or that way or that, if I had this or that, I could more easily achieve what I want, but there is always uncertainty, for the simple reason that we do not dare to make things happen. It is undeniable that as human beings we will always be tested, but it is the way we handle them that makes the difference. Being aware of my weaknesses is my first big step towards strengthening my character and becoming part of those who make things happen.

If I recognize that I have taken a negative stance toward life, toward others, and that I may not have been interested in cultivating good relationships where both sides win, it is a step of honesty with myself that leads me to transcend those limits that have kept me from seeing beyond my self-centeredness. Recognizing my failures and renewing my way of thinking is to evolve. It's starting to give meaning to my life. It's being aware that from my thoughts I'm creating what I want to see.

"The outer world reflects the state of the inner world. By controlling one's thoughts and the way one reacts to life's events, one begins to control one's destiny." Robin S. Sharma

Naturally, human beings are prone to make mistakes, but continuing to fail at the same task over and over again keeps us at a standstill. The interest in constant improvement is the flame that must be fed daily, if we really want to obtain new results.

Usually the people in our family, who are our closest environment, are the ones who know about our behaviors and attitudes; however, only we know if we are being authentic or if we are wearing a mask in front of others. The point is, how do we really act when no one is looking? Or how do we behave with those around us?

I think many of us have heard comments about how when couples get married, after a while they change. I really think it's not that one or the other has changed over time, but rather that when they first met, they may not have shown their personality sincerely.

Being honest with myself first and showing others how I am, with my strengths and weaknesses, allows me to gain the trust of others in a transparent way and not to satisfy my own interests. Additionally, I would be giving others the opportunity to choose me for who I am and not for what I may appear to be. In any case, the true essence of each individual sooner or later comes to light and with it, the results.

It would be much better to be able to express ourselves in all honesty when something is not working well and to work together in the search for positive changes that will lead us to individual and collective growth.

Recognizing when we have failed is a sign of humility and courage, because many times it is not so easy to assume our mistakes. Our tendency is almost always to point out and free ourselves from any responsibility, as this is easier.

Being honest with myself and assuming that I have areas to focus on in order to improve them opens up a field of possibilities that will be useful to me in that process. These possibilities can be manifested through people, situations or things that will come at the right time and in the right place, just to help us find the perfect path. (It can be a book, a message or perhaps a call from someone).

Being willing to invest time to know our personality and to grow as individuals, gives us the privilege of enjoying a better quality of life and enables us to positively influence others.

Walking through a place we know well gives us security and confidence, but first we had to walk through it, suddenly not just once, but many times. The same could be said about human beings. Each one of us is like a huge garden waiting to be discovered.

Many walk the path of existence without having any knowledge of themselves, so they do not know what decision to make in the face of adverse circumstances, neither do they know what is the right direction to continue their journey. In situations like these, it is when assuming the position of victim is the easiest thing. To think that everything is happening because of external causes, when we should be making the decision to take responsibility for our own destiny.

Every time we go into our own being and detail ourselves carefully, we become the observer who knows what is in there in that wonderful manifestation of the Universe. Keeping our thinking under continuous self-observation generates an effect that elevates us to a higher level of consciousness and therefore promotes a healthier and calmer life.

The more we work on improving as people, the more productive each task we perform becomes, and the more tranquility and love we radiate. Many people will want to be imbued with our good vibrations. The lens through which we observe life becomes clearer, we begin to see that all is well. Our environment becomes a place of rest and peace. A splendid place that brings joy and security. All this and much more can be transmitted from our mind, knowing the creative potential of our thoughts.

By recognizing our mistakes or weaknesses, we acquire the ability to understand others. We become more compassionate, as we come to understand that just as we are weak in some areas, others may be weak in others, and so I return to that true version of myself.

Recognizing weaknesses and also wanting to change, allows us to experience great satisfaction, because it requires determination and work to change those habits with which we have always lived. Many times we will continue to make mistakes, even after being aware of them, but longing for change and striving to be better will make change possible. It is an absolutely rewarding experience. These challenges make us test our potential and convince us that all goals can be achieved if we give our best effort.

By observing ourselves, we deeply discover who we are. It allows us to perceive all those strengths we have within us and all the creativity we can develop, which have suddenly gone unnoticed by us and obviously by others.

Stopping to judge the behavior of others is a waste of time, since this does not help at all, it only delays the progress towards our personal growth.

If we identify our strengths, we can take advantage of them, focusing them towards the achievement of our projects. Let us remember that each of us is endowed with skills that we must discover and know how to use for the benefit of all. It is important to base these skills on integrity and humility.

My intention when writing about the weaknesses and strengths we may have as people, is to express that good or bad are nothing more than concepts which exist in the mind of each one of us. Each person has a different view of life. Everyone has certain references in their mind and acts accordingly. That is where our prudence should excel so that we do not exercise judgment against anyone or anything; for each person is free to express their thoughts.

The same can be said with regard to the customs of each region or country. They are neither good nor bad, they are only the concepts or information with which we were taught and which have been transmitted from generation to generation. What is important to emphasize is that there are principles or rules of life that favor healthy coexistence, which we can put into practice, regardless of cultures or concepts of each community. We are not alone in this world and we need each other. No one could emerge without the help of others. As an example of this we can take the idea of: "what I do not want to be done to me, I will not do to others". By applying this principle I am getting to know myself. From that position I not only improve my relationships, but I manage to strengthen myself as an integral person who generates harmony. I begin to be part of a positive change. I would be contributing so that our society, or at least the surrounding community, is a friendly environment, where love and creativity abound, where good values are practiced and where we are interested not only in our own well-being, but also in that of our fellow human beings.

In our social environment we can work as entrepreneurs, parents, employees or any other profession, but what really gives it an added value is the way we assume these functions. It depends on each one of us if we carry out our tasks in excellence or on the contrary we do them only to fulfill or for the need to generate an income.

When we start from the thought **"I am my first reviewer"**, we are being honest with ourselves. Not only do the people we serve benefit, but we also get privileges that we never thought we would get. In addition, there is satisfaction in doing the work well out of conviction.

All work is important in a community. For example, in a company, the president is as important as the cleaner or the messenger. All of them are essential for the company to remain strong. So much so, that you usually meet the receptionist first, rather than the president. She is part of the image of the company and if she does not perform her job with the necessary quality, it could generate customer dissatisfaction or even the loss of good business for the company.

A company can lose customers because of the way they answer the phone. Similarly, it can find new business opportunities, just by providing excellent service and the kindness with which they attend. There are people who have joined a company to perform a position classified as simple and gradually move up to administrative positions. In many cases, they become important businessmen, because they are determined to put their skills at the service of others and because they know how to take advantage of the opportunities that arise.

When we develop work focusing our strengths on serving with excellence, we are giving ourselves the opportunity to leave traces of blessing wherever we go; in addition to gaining the admiration and respect of the people we serve, our mind will be recharged with satisfaction for all the positive attitudes we decide to generate towards others.

A strength is a reference point of who we are. It is a virtue, for which we can be recognized. It is our decision how we want to be remembered in the places we go. Always in function of being part of the change.

It is through our strengths and virtues that we can carry out the plans we make for ourselves. It is our duty to examine ourselves internally and discover the qualities that will help us renew our habits and consequently give a better focus to our objectives.

It is necessary to develop our abilities and although it is challenging it is possible to achieve. We can talk for example about self-discipline, which after being developed, facilitates the practice of new habits that make our life go from ordinary to extraordinary.

We feel good when we achieve a personal accomplishment, even if it is not meaningful to anyone but ourselves. If others applaud and enjoy it, it is an additional pleasure because it could be shared, but if no one notices, it has to be equally satisfying and productive.

Knowing that we have certain strengths will always motivate us to want to go further, to dream bigger things and something much better such as inspiring someone else to risk doing something that they have wanted to do and that out of fear had not dared to do. It's nice to know that the decision to know myself influences my environment to be better and that new possibilities are created.

The purpose of this book is to provide ideas that bring us closer to the knowledge of ourselves, to make us aware of that potential that is inside us and that we must discover to increase our quality of life. We must also understand that a community is made up of individuals, of which we are also part of.

Such participation can build or destroy, hate or love, hurt or heal. We all have the creative power from our thoughts. We generate change from within. We can be part of those who see an abundant and sufficient panorama for all, in which it is not necessary that in order for one to obtain something, another must be deprived of it. We are all endowed with the same creative power and we can all access the abundant riches that the Universe, God or Source (whatever you prefer to call it) has to give.

Strengths and weaknesses make up our personal balance and we can use them to our advantage. If we focus the skills we possess to correct the supposed errors that have kept us from moving forward, we gain in experience and that is something that can only be achieved by experiencing it. We begin to make sense of life in a different way. Our perception of the world changes for the better. We notice changes around us that motivate us to improve more and more. It is not by chance that we find people who smile at us and express kindness to us. All this will be the result of our actions and the way we have renewed our thoughts. We may also begin to notice that people like to be close to us. A series of events that will work to our benefit will become more frequent. Even situations that previously seemed unfavorable to us, we can now see them as part of our training and as an opportunity to experience ourselves in a different way.

Every time a seed is sown, there is a harvest. The harvest is always greater. It is an unbreakable universal law. The same goes for us; we reap what we sow.

What kind of seed are you sowing?

Whatever we do, the results will surely be reflected in ourselves.

We might take an indigent person as an example; chances are their results will not be the most productive in terms of goals. Or how about someone who acts dishonestly? - Surely the effects will be reflected in their relationships and in their economy. In the same way we can generate positive effects that bring benefits to ourselves and others, starting in our thoughts. Therefore, if we take care now to correct our mistakes, undoubtedly our quality of life in the future will have to be much better.

It is a challenge to recognize that we are wrong, that we have certain areas that need to be renewed, but many times we do not see our successes, (nor do we celebrate the small triumphs) when it is those small triumphs that lead us to achieve greater things.

Let's risk looking at ourselves face to face in the mirror to discover that immense inner panorama we possess. Let's recognize the things to improve and even more all those qualities we have that add value to our life. Starting from this point of applying the knowledge acquired, our world has to change. We will feel capable of assuming adverse situations with greater peace of mind, since there will be enough awareness in us to identify between what we know is difficult to control and what we already master easily. We will know what we must do at a certain moment so that circumstances do not bring us down and so that problems do not stop us in the race to reach our dreams.

Making mistakes is human, but continuing to make them and not being willing to remedy them can cause a lot of frustration. If we identify them and put effort into trying to correct them, focusing our strengths towards that goal, we will open doors that we didn't even imagine existed.

"The man who knows himself has in his hand the key that opens all the doors to his own universe."

"There's only one small part of the universe that you know, for sure, can be improved and that part is you." Aldous Huxley

CHAPTER THREE
Security and Self-Confidence

Triumphs and defeats exist only in the mind of the one who lives them. It is in our mind where strong battles are unleashed and it is right there where many times they are lost without even having been given the opportunity to fight them; but how can we achieve this if we have so many fears that do not allow us to think that we can win, that we can achieve success and that we can also go as far as our mind allows?

It is remarkable to see how weaknesses dominate strengths. Small weaknesses cause great frustrations in human beings, and powerful strengths remain undiscovered, due to insecurity and not believing in ourselves.

Insecurity is a common weakness in human beings. In most cases it is acquired in childhood; it is learned from the environment, due to the ignorance of adults when they tell us: you are going to fall! Don't do this or that! Don't put on those clothes, you look ridiculous!

Disempowering expressions like these are common in the formation of many children. Perhaps at some point we were teased by friends about some physical trait, about our name, or simply about something we didn't do well; as a result of the teasing, we used insecurity as a defense mechanism and began to act out of expectation of external approval.

All this information is becoming part of our culture and is being passed on from generation to generation.

In childhood, we soak up everything we see and hear around us like sponges. We want to know everything; we are curious about everything and we are always ready to do whatever allows us to enjoy every moment. At this point, the wisdom of parents is paramount to guide their children and prepare them to face life. It should be a teaching that allows the child to grow up feeling happy, but above all feeling that it has the capacity to face and resolve every circumstance that life brings. It is the parents' responsibility to be aware of the way they educate their children and what kind of values they instill in them so that they learn to live in community; moreover, something very important is to analyze the talents that each child has, in order to help them to potentialize and develop them.

To be a father is to assume responsibility for the life of your children, understanding that according to the formation and example received in childhood, it is what will most certainly mark their quality of life when they grow up. A good formation is fundamental, since it will provide the necessary tools to learn to assume their own life with responsibility.

As we grow up, life places us in different scenarios where what we learn will be put into practice.

Where our attitudes will allow us to transcend the circumstances in spite of how strong they are, or on the contrary where we collapse and prefer to blame others because we do not know what decision to make, or how to assume that moment.

A child could grow up being aware that life is made up of ups and downs. It is a reality that does not have to be hidden. Many times things will not go as planned, but the lived experience will be the springboard that will give the impulse to other, even bigger, projects. There will always be opportunities for new attempts, the challenges will be greater and greater but the skills will also be up to the task of overcoming them.

These concepts are fundamental in a child's education. Parents are primarily responsible and are fortunate to be able to pass them on.

Any fear and insecurity within each of us, whether it was produced in our childhood or in any situation experienced at any stage of life, cannot be an excuse not to face them. It is our responsibility to address it and we must do so without judgment. It is necessary to understand that those people who in some way influenced us negatively, acted from their formation and their level of consciousness. It is a chain, which each one of us can break.

Passing judgment on others because of the way we were taught or influenced does not change the situation. It is better to have the determination to let go of the past, to release that weight and heal our heart. Then we will move more quickly toward our other purposes. This wise decision to move forward without guilt and judgment will allow us to see all that we can achieve when we take the reins of our life with responsibility.

Security and self-confidence, a phrase containing great meaning when it comes to enjoying a good life.

It is easy to recognize a person when they are sure of themselves, without having to be very close to them; it is a quality that becomes very noticeable. This stands out in the way they speak, in the tone of their voice, in the way they express themselves and in their movements. This security generates very positive expectations in all the fields in which the person develops. This is why confidence becomes a key card for us and if for some reason we lost it at some point in our lives, this is the perfect opportunity to start recovering it.

It's time to turn that order of priorities we've been focusing on around and then we'll find ourselves taking another big step on our road to happiness.

We have already become aware that both what we are and what we have are a result of our inner self. We now know that we can search within our own minds to discover that security and confidence we possess and how we can use it to our advantage. It is an acquired knowledge that can be put into practice little by little, until it becomes a habit. It is one thing to have knowledge and quite another to put it into practice. The decision to generate new results is in the hands of each one of us. If you not only receive it in your mind, but in your heart and analyze if you are really willing to improve whatever needs to be improved to achieve what you want in your life, then you will discover that you are a winner. The humility to recognize our mistakes makes us great human beings who are constantly growing.

The security and confidence in ourselves allows us to go beyond the conventional limits. The self-confident person throws themselves into giving the best in everything they do. Those who are insecure prefer to be in certainty, even if they are left behind so as not to face the pressure.

Insecurity makes us stingy in a way, because although we have the best to give, we don't do it out of fear. Minimum effort is given and therefore one cannot receive in abundance. Insecurity encourages the habit of conformity. An insecure person lacks identity and character; that explains why he does what others tell him to do or what he sees others doing. He acts in accordance to the masses.

A confident person does not get absorbed into the system easily. They do not fall into the trap of living by what they say or looking good to others. A self-confident person thinks, speaks and acts according to his principles and his own criteria. They know that if they make a mistake in their decision, they can try again and they are sure to get better results. The self-confident person is not guided by the materialism that the system wants to engender in our minds, since he knows that even physical beauty is transient (although when a person beautifies himself within, that beauty is naturally exteriorized). His confidence is not placed in material goods because he understands that they come and go. The person who trusts in himself does not lean into consumerism; he is not wrapped in the threads of vanity, pride and arrogance.

Being confident allows us to be humble, to project ourselves in a simple and pleasant way before other people. That security drives us to always give the best according to our abilities. It definitely puts us in privileged places. Giving more than we are used to allows us to be part of the change we want to see.

By challenging ourselves, we achieve excellence at our own discretion; keeping in mind that being excellent is not being perfect, but it is making the decision to do things better and better (conscientiously). In this way the objectives we set for ourselves will become more visible and real.

Every human being runs his own race. Some go ahead and others behind, but each one runs his own race and faces his own obstacles. We will always see people who achieve very great things and others not so great. Let us keep in mind that each person exists for a different purpose.

If for some reason we fall, and there will probably come a time like this, there will always be two options: to get up and continue until our purpose is fulfilled or to decide not to do so. The attitude of strength and security will be decisive in the achievement of any objective. There is something that is an important part of our life and it is **the motivation** that makes us wake up every day in high spirits. Since it is not just living for the sake of living, it is living with the awareness that everything that can be dreamed of, can be achieved. It is also wonderful to know that we can motivate others to achieve their goals as well and celebrate them as if they were our own. The Universe has reserves for everyone and in abundance. It all depends on the aspirations that each person has in their mind and how willing they are to give the best of themselves, in the achievement of those goals.

Motivation is the fuel that makes us deeply yearn for a goal. For this reason our daily habits should be inspiring and uplifting. It is up to us to keep that spark burning.

Stop for a moment and analyze what is the motivation of your life, what moves the fibers of your being, what you are passionate about regardless of the approval of others.

When you begin to define these priorities, you also begin to give your life a direction. We gain clarity about who we really are, we know where we come from and how far we could go. A universe of opportunity begins to unfold before our eyes. We find faculties in ourselves that had not even crossed our minds and everything acquires a new meaning.

Taking quality time to get to know ourselves, to be alone and to listen to the voice of the heart, makes our character assert itself and we begin to see life from another perspective. New ideas will come and new projects will motivate us to work on them.

If you focus on achieving that confidence in yourself and in your abilities, you will learn to throw yourself into the void without fear of losing.

A person who longs to find their security takes advantage of their moments of solitude and recreation to practice personal growth rituals and knows that it is there where they find all the answers to their dilemmas. It is in that connection with their inner self that they are filled with security and confidence for all they can do and achieve on their own. This type of person understands that they are not alone, since they feel at their best and also when they are surrounded by other people they always have interesting things to contribute, they make others feel welcome and can enjoy pleasant moments.

When a person does not believe in themselves, they often lack the tact to socialize with others and are prone to be upset by insignificant details. If something is not to their liking, no matter how small, it is a big problem. They are reckless in expressing their opinions about other people's ideas. They believe that everything should be done their own way and think that they have the absolute truth of things.

Those who believe in themselves respect the ideas of others, even if they do not agree with them. They know how to reach out to people with kindness and charisma; they know how to live in community. They are calm people who are not easily destabilized by external causes.

They are always well dressed and wear what they like, not so that someone can see them, but because they know they deserve the best. Their physical appearance is carefully managed for their own satisfaction. The confident person cultivates values and good interpersonal relationships. At their workplace, they are not petty. They do not just do what they are paid to do, but they feel capable of running the extra mile. The self-confident person has high thoughts, has the facility to perceive their environment the way they want to see it, because they know that change begins in their mind. It is always a matter of giving the best that you can.

Their confidence makes them capable of facing great challenges. Whatever work they do they can make it the best way to prove to themselves and, in turn, to other, that they are excellent at what they do. That's their secret touch. We have powerful tools, including **our creativity and our attitude.** They are what make what we do beautiful and great. This is a very valuable point to keep in mind when undertaking any work.

Security and self-confidence contain a whole chain of values shaped by love and passion. When we do what we are passionate about, we are already successful because we are living by conviction and this brings about infallible results.

To be sure of oneself is to maintain emotional balance. It is to be free from dependence on what people will say, from perhaps having to live hidden behind someone who is not authentic, for fear of not being accepted.

Let us look at the extent to which insecurity has led human beings to the point of losing their lives because of dissatisfaction with their bodies. Many men and women enter an operating room trying to raise their self-esteem without realizing that it is they themselves who have not accepted themselves to begin with. What they reflect is their inner world and they will always find a new dissatisfaction to fill if they do not work on their confidence from the inside out and not the other way around. The only way to acquire security and confidence is to accept ourselves as we are and work on our weaknesses from within; otherwise there will always be a dependency on something external keeping us enslaved to insecurity.

If the belief that physical beauty, money or material things were synonymous with happiness, then would only some have access to it?. And every time one of these factors was missing, would happiness also end?

Self-confidence produces in a person the capacity to assimilate to all the circumstances of their life, however difficult they may be, with greater serenity and integrity.

Security connects with a valuable part of our being such as *integrity*, that way of doing the right thing, even when no one sees us.

Acquiring self-confidence is a process, we should not pretend to have achieved everything in the blink of an eye; it requires commitment and dedication, but it is possible to achieve it. Giving yourself the opportunity to look into your life and believe that it is possible to achieve, is already a big step.

The world is full of men and women adapted to living in a common condition. That is to say, people who go without a defined direction or purpose. Without identity, without character (unconscious). People who act moved by what they see (emotions) and not by their own conviction. They easily give up their dreams for fear of what others will say or worse, they don't even have dreams. Those who do not dream miss the opportunity to materialize great things in their lives. Dreams keep us alive. Dreams motivate us to get up every day and move forward until we achieve them. Dreaming is not sitting around waiting for everything to be perfect so that we can finally have a happy life, that's a delusion. Dreaming is visualizing in our mind first, but it is also opening our eyes in the morning, thanking God, the Creator or Universal Mind (depending on your spiritual belief) for life, for the opportunity of a new day when I make the decision on how to live it. It is to be aware that my attitude is decisive in any circumstance that may arise. That if I get up early I can make my day more productive. To dream is to know how to manage time. It is preparing myself from the morning to give my best to whatever I do; at home, at work, on the street. It is not the work or the people around me that generate my well-being, it comes from me. The outside world is the result of my inner world. Everything I observe in my environment is my own reflection. It depends on the perspective with which I see at things. There is no excuse not to make today the best day of my life.

No one is to blame for what happens to us, our security allows us to assume that responsibility as our own. We have the power to raise our thoughts to the top and see a landscape full of opportunities. It is only up to us to see doors open where others see them closed. Today we must realize that we have the potential, enough talent and capability to be better people, to be better at home, to be efficient in the places where we work, to be better bosses, to be better friends. Each and every one of us is capable, perfectly gifted and equipped with everything we need to live happily on this earth.

Security is that something inside you that gives you a special strength. That something that tells you that you deserve a peaceful and happy life. It is that feeling that everything is fine, that there is nothing to worry about. It is a thought that there is nothing you cannot achieve. It is an inner feeling of firmness that is reflected externally in your upright back and your calm, deep breath. Security is part of you and it never left. It's just that if you lost it at some point during your life, it's here and now that you're ready to find it again.

In conclusion, I want to tell you not to get discouraged thinking that there are too many things to improve. Even if you think it won't be easy, it is possible to do it. You just have to go step by step, enjoying the process. Without hurry, but without pause, with all the effort and the desire to enjoy a full life in spite of the circumstances. Self-confidence will allow you to see that it is easier than you thought.

When we learn to live only one day at a time, without being tied to the past, no matter how good or bad it was, or to the future, since it is uncertain (although it is important to prepare ourselves to have a good future, we still do not know what will happen), we will be taking a leap that will allow us to start living a more harmonious and peaceful life. For this reason, let us learn to live our beautiful life in the present moment, aware of the here and now. Let us live with wisdom, always with the best attitude. Let's talk less and listen more. Let's focus more attention on our inner confidence. I recommend you to set up a simple project about the way you think it will be easiest for you to strengthen your personal security and write it down on a piece of paper. I assure you that you will have very positive results and you will realize that when one reaches a goal, no matter how small, it automatically stimulates us to project ourselves towards a bigger one.

CHAPTER FOUR
"Identity and Character"

In my personal concept, I believe that identity has to do with the essence of the person. It's that set of characteristics that makes us unique.

Character is the impetus with which we act and of course it's part of our identity.

Based on the definition of these two words, we will try to focus on discovering if the identity that manifests itself through my way of being is my true identity or if on the contrary I assumed it, according to the information I received from the environment in which I grew up (family, school, church, friends, others).

Many times the fear of losing something or someone, the fear of being in the crosshairs of criticism, the fear of risking a relationship or simply the fear of being excluded from a certain social circle leads us to bend our way of thinking. How many times do we stop expressing what we really feel the way we would like to and end up saying what others want to hear? It is something very simple and common, but it should not be like that, because each person has the right to express himself freely according to his own convictions.

It is important for us to be clear that identity and character have nothing to do with competing with others, but rather with authenticity and integrity.

Every person has the ability to discover within themselves their true identity even if it has long been hidden behind a shell imposed by society. This encounter with one's identity will allow one to become a truly authentic being.

This authenticity will give them the ability to appreciate things from their own perspective. You will not be easily moved by other people's ideas or by the system (obviously, without entering into controversy with anyone). Your conviction will keep you motivated, and your focused thinking will result in firmness of character.

As for integrity, one could say that it is linked to character, since both are associated with the idea that we are what we are, regardless of whether we are observed or not. In other words, being authentic and honest allows us to experience a different way of life, where I am my own observer and by my own will, I act with transparency. Each one of us is the owner of a genuine essence and it is precisely this essence that makes us unique and immensely valuable.

However, let us keep in mind that the idea is not to impose our opinions as an absolute truth since it does not exist as such, let alone to ignore other people's freedom of expression.

Let us remember the importance of freeing ourselves from the concepts of good and bad. We need to learn to respect the thoughts and lives of others.

When we are afraid of being criticized, we are reluctant to express our feelings naturally, putting our self-confidence into play. It is this insecurity that bends us into action, waiting for the approval of others, thus manifesting frustration and resentment.

All the information that fills our minds defines who we are. Everything we see and hear strongly influences the life we lead. Everything we express comes from a thought. The mind is full of memories that correspond to everything we have perceived throughout our lives, voluntarily or involuntarily. Everything that comes out of us is because at some point it entered our mind. For this reason, we must be attentive to the information that we allow to enter our brain and in the same way be aware of everything that we also transmit to others.

Let's carefully review the kind of lyrics contained in the music we listen to, the kind of videos we are used to watching, the information that reaches our electronic devices, the kind of programs we watch and the kind of people we interact with.

Is it really worth the time we're spending on all this kind of information? Is it bringing something into our lives that will allow us to grow as people and have a harmonious and prosperous life?

When a person loses their identity and character, they become a weather vane that is easily blown by whatever subtle wind it may be. The person who is weak in character allows his dignity to be trampled upon, loses credibility in the eyes of others, lets themselves be carried away by the masses, falls into deception and often gives in to the desires of others without expressing his point of view.

We are used to hearing and saying that bad company corrupts good habits and this is true in a way, but if you have a defined identity and character you will not easily succumb to those things that we know do not generate something positive.

Having character should never be focused on imposing a criterion, but its main function will be to keep us focused on everything that connects us to remaining firm in achieving the goals we set and become mirrors that motivate others to seek their true essence.

Each person is unique and possesses great virtues, enough to achieve everything in life. This is the best time to reflect on your identity and character; perhaps you have not allowed them to shine as they should. Without knowing it, perhaps we have been living the lives of others for some time and not our own.

That vulnerability is more latent in the absence of the will and strength required to freely express our thoughts.

Many times we are induced to do things that will bring serious problems to our lives, because we do not have that firmness of character to say **"no"** in time. In addition, when a person has no identity, they don't know what to do or what to say in certain important moments of their life; that's why they prefer to let themselves be carried away by the decisions that others make and at the moment in which they have to assume the consequences of their decisions, which were made unconsciously, is when the excuses, the faults, the regrets begin to arrive and, in the worst scenario, there will be no time for regrets.

The lack of identity delays our achievements because we are afraid to express our own ideas. It makes us uncomfortable to be in the spotlight, we avoid failure and so we do not even dare to try. Time passes quickly, and when we least expect it, we have wasted too much time due to lack of decision.

In identity and character is the source of where decisions are made in our lives. It is where determination becomes latent. It is there that good ideas flow and are set in motion. A person with a defined identity always knows what decision to make at the right time. They have a clear sense of direction. They do not deviate from their goals. They stand firmly by their beliefs, even if they are different from others. A person with an identity leads by example, since his or her character allows him or her to achieve the goals set. They always win because even when things don't go as expected, they know that every experience has a purpose. For those who have identity and character, obstacles are motivation to continue. Firmness of character allows you to act on your own conviction and even if you make your own arguments with confidence, you do not fall into the trap of judging others based on their mindset or way of life. It is always to the benefit of healthy coexistence.

As integral beings, it is vitally important that we understand that just as there is food to nourish the physical body, there is also food to nourish the mind. Being the mind as important as the body, since from our thoughts, our external world is created.

We can find foods that fill up the body, but do not really nourish it. The same happens with what we absorb through what we see and hear; we nourish our life or on the contrary we only fill it up with information that in the end does not help us to progress in our process of growth and evolution.

All human beings are born with an original identity and a character, but as we grow physically, these are changed

by the information that constantly reaches us. We could say that it is impossible to keep them intact and grow with that natural essence, but it is possible to keep it a little more, if parents take greater responsibility for the formation of their children.

Similarly, it is possible to recover identity and character in adulthood, the difference is that we are already responsible for turning our own lives around. Awareness is essential in order to act and begin to know our own being. In this way, a new opportunity for life begins to unfold before us.

Whatever our life projection is, it is possible to achieve it. There must only be coherence between our thoughts and our actions, to put our knowledge into practice and encourage others to move forward on their path as well. All this is part of our identity and character and of our true essence. *As I think, so I act and live.*

If identity and character are well founded in our lives, we are able to handle each circumstance that comes our way with more fortitude. We can be autonomous in our decisions and therefore we will not allow ourselves to be diverted from our projections and objectives regardless of the pressure from our environment.

Being an ordinary person does not mean being "in", it is a sign that perhaps one lacks identity; for one does what others do only because not being accepted causes fear. It means that it takes character to decide for yourself.

If that's the case, then it would be better to be "out", because I would be showing myself that I am valuable, spontaneous and natural, that I have a conviction of my own and that I am not interested in looking good in front of others. It's about standing firm in my ideals. Not letting myself be dragged down by the currents of the system. Getting out of the enslavement of having to do what the masses do.

Many of us have come to feel sad at times about not being accepted by others, when we should be the first to accept ourselves no matter what they say or think about us.

The information provided by the "media" has become a general rule. It seems that they are the ones in charge of pointing out the path we should all walk. To wear our hair in a certain way, to have the ideal figure of the body based on measures stipulated by them, the clothes, the food, etc. All of this is simply a cultural transmission and if we are not strengthened in our conviction, in one way or another they will end up impacting our lives unfavorably. .

It is time to stop and analyze your current life. Reflect on the way you have been performing your role. How are you managing your time, what are the goals you have achieved and what would you like to achieve? Do you have autonomy over your thoughts or do others decide for you?.

If we ask someone else about their life, according to their answers we get an idea of what it is like and what kind of life they have. The same happens if we ask ourselves, and with even more reason, since we are the ones who know our own secrets.

Self-examination causes an inner revolution since it allows us to be honest and aware of our own reality. It allows us to proceed responsibly and take control of our actions. Obviously, we need to take time to develop this habit. There is one practice that is very simple, but it has a very positive impact and that is to stand in front of the mirror and look into our eyes. Discovering ourselves, facing the fear of seeing what we do not like about our body and accepting it with gratitude. You will see how you become empowered and how you gain confidence in yourself. You will be able to look into the eyes of others and transmit confidence.

Looking into each other's eyes seems like a simple exercise, but it helps to cross that barrier that has kept us away from our identity and our essence. It's starting to generate the encounter with my true nature. That's where the change in my life will really start... when I meet my true self.

To find my true identity is to get to the starting point, just before I have received all that information that covered my true self. It's discovering my qualities and my potential. Knowing what I like to do, what I do best, what my virtues are and how I can put them at the service of others. It is also to identify weak areas that have limited me and work on them to turn them into strengths or at least learn to control them and have self-control. It is to have the courage to recognize my negative attitudes and transform them into new creative ideas that contribute to my integral growth.

I can start by learning to remove all the disempowering information from my mind and replace it with information that sets my creative mind in motion with new thoughts.

Replace those old, rusty, and repetitive thoughts that we have been generating in our minds for years and years with powerful thoughts that motivate us to believe that everything can be better. That whatever I dream, I can achieve. That I can improve interpersonal relationships and perhaps, why not, forgive someone who hurt us in the past. In short, it is to begin to free ourselves from things that we have carried for a long time and that now we have the opportunity to let go of. It is to start smiling more often, to embrace even unknown people, to be silent when it is necessary and to speak at the right time.

Putting yourself in the other person's place will always allow you to understand a little more every situation and see it from another perception. Every reaction to a circumstance in life is marked by previous information that guides us to act accordingly. It is here that through character, we decide to start renewing those old patterns of behavior that have kept us stagnant and unhappy.

Each circumstance has the option of being interpreted with a negative attitude which will make the problems bigger, or with a positive and intelligent attitude which will definitely bring solutions and harmony for everyone.

"You are seeing what you want to see. You are the master of interpreting things your way." - A course in miracles

Discovering my identity connects me with spontaneity; with that authentic and natural being that is me, regardless of what others think, but it also reminds me of the sense of respect for each person's way of being and thinking; understanding that others don't have to be like me or like I would expect them to be. There is nothing good or bad, just different ways of perceiving life. That is freedom of thought.

Finding your identity will allow you to become a calm person, since you will not have to do or stop doing anything to please others. You will not be afraid of losing friends if you do not do the same things they do. You will simply learn to enjoy being yourself, begin to love yourself more and feel joyful about your life. If you find yourself alone or accompanied, you will still feel at ease.

Being alone will no longer be a cause for concern because when you renew your outlook on life, you become a magnet for good relationships.

We will conclude this chapter by emphasizing the importance of reviewing, with honesty ,who we have been up to now and who we really are. Understanding that there was information that covered our essence and if we truly long to see a radical transformation in everything that makes up our life today, we ourselves are called to rediscover our true identity.

Let us remember that free will allows us to decide our own life. Many people do not use it because they allow themselves to be captivated by the traps of the system, such as social networks, television, fashions and all the media that are used today to manipulate people's minds without allowing them to think for themselves. A person with a defined identity and character allows only that which drives them to grow and evolve as an individual being into their life and as a result becomes a great contribution to society.

CHAPTER FIVE
"Meeting my life's purpose"

I sincerely hope that at this point, you have been putting into practice the principles learned in the previous chapters, because this will make it much easier for us to find our life's purpose and all that it represents.

In a simple way, I could define the purpose as the *"What for" of my existence.* The reason we came to this earthly plane.

Within every human manifestation there is a reason for being and that is the responsibility of each of us, to discover what it is.

Everything that happens in our life has a certain purpose, nothing happens by chance and everything is linked to what we need in our process of evolution. It all depends on the level of commitment we make to personal growth.

Consciously, let's look at these two times: ***past and future.*** The past is behind us, however wonderful or difficult it may have been, and it will never come back. While it is true that there are sweet memories that make our present happy, there are also bitter ones that even bring tears to our eyes, even if they happened a long time ago. However, looking at the past, in one way or another, will only delay our personal development. To remember sad or difficult moments is to waste our valuable time on something we can no longer change. You cannot look at two sides at once. Either you look at one side or you look at the other. It's your choice.

Staring at the past will keep us distracted and away from living consciously in the present. The same goes for the future, which is definitely uncertain. And even though we already have the knowledge that our tomorrow will be the result of the way we think, speak and act today, we are not sure what will happen anyway. If for a moment we devote ourselves to thinking consciously about some circumstance in which we find ourselves living now, whatever it may be, it is the result of our past actions. It is impossible to break the universal law that says, *"what we sow is what we reap, but in greater quantity."*

Depending on how we live today, that's the quality of life we'll have tomorrow. Of course, we must prepare for a promising future and make our long-term projections, because they motivate us and inject us with that extra fuel to move forward every day, although each day will come in an unexpected way.

Where will we be tomorrow? What kind of activities will we be doing? There are many possibilities and moments that we have to live, but none of them are certain to come. It does not mean that we are assuming a negative position, we are thinking coherently about what can happen later. It is for this precise reason, for the uncertainty that the past and the future sometimes cause us, that we need to make an effort to learn to be in the moment so that we do not miss the pleasure of enjoying the road we are on.

We must live life in real time. Real time is today. All we need to understand is that each day brings its own dilemmas, but also all the solutions. As we read in the previous chapter, every circumstance has two paths that will always depend on our decision and that decision will end up affecting our future. The more wisely we live in the present, the more prosperous and peaceful our days will be in the future.

We must make every effort to make each moment the best yet. Let us take the good out of every circumstance and look for new and better alternatives that will lead us to transform any adverse situation into an opportunity for growth. Let our imagination fly towards all that is good and constructive. Let's use our free will and decide to enjoy life to the fullest, regardless of what we call problems (remember that problems are only in the mind of those who believe they have them. We should see every circumstance as an opportunity for learning and growth, adhering to the solutions).

"Every adversity, every failure, every pain carries within it the seed of an equivalent or greater benefit." - Napoleon Hill

We would be lying if we said that the day would come when we would not go through difficult times again, but what is certain is that if we learn to face those situations that overwhelm us, with a good attitude and with gratitude, the most likely outcome is that we will land on top and with the satisfaction of having passed the test. Every time we overcome obstacles along the way, we become stronger and calmer. We are acquiring the strength to take on great challenges in our lives. In addition to this, we begin to acquire confidence in ourselves because we know we have the capacity to accept situations with maturity and the courage to put our face to the breeze.

We were all born as part of a divine purpose. That purpose is that we live happily on this earth and that we can serve and motivate the people around us to be happy.

Is it possible to discover my life's purpose? Yes, of course it is!

It is possible to find it when we make the decision to know ourselves and look inside ourselves for that something for which we were put in this paradise called earth. To know myself is to know the ground on which I walk, and this definitely gives me great security.

Looking inside ourselves to assume that there are areas of our life that need to be renewed and make the decision to change, brings as a result fluidity in our daily lives. Everything begins to fit perfectly when we enter into that awareness that leads us to perceive life from a different perspective, in which we assume the responsibility that everything we are is a result of ourselves; eliminating all kinds of excuses and guilt towards others.

To live a life with purpose is to know where I am going, it is to know that I have the possibility to set goals for myself and work until I reach them. Living with purpose produces a great motivation to get up every morning, because we know that there is a goal we are heading for and that reaching that goal brings satisfaction to our lives. It is very important that we keep in mind that our life's purpose is fully linked to service to others and to our commitment to create a better world.

Walking in our life's purpose allows us to help those we meet along the way. It is a wonderful way to draw blessings to ourselves. Each person gives of what they have inside, and we all have very valuable things to share. Each individual has special virtues that at some point can become an important help to other people, but sometimes selfishness keeps us distracted, thinking about everything we do not have and what we need, which does not let us see the needs of others, when there is so much we can give to our society, whether it is family, friends, neighbors, co-workers or study colleagues. We just need to stop and pay attention; we will realize that sometimes a single word of encouragement, a smile or simply a kind gesture, can change a person's life. It is fundamental to recognize the value of knowing that other people also need to move forward and maybe I can become that support for them to reach the top of their own life and their own dreams.

By helping others, we are applying the principle of giving. To serve from the heart in a selfless way is already reason enough to feel satisfied.

On the other hand, to serve or to help, expecting to receive something in return, could be disconcerting. We may even lose the motivation to continue, if the people we help do not give back to us in the way we expect. Giving and doing so only for personal satisfaction can result in pleasant and unexpected rewards. It is interesting at this point to emphasize that giving is not only linked to material things, since each person gives of what he or she has. As we said before, we all have something good to contribute, whether it is a hug, good advice, a kind gesture, a moment to listen, a prayer and many other contributions that we could mention and that can truly become the support of someone who needs it at a certain moment.

There are many ways in which we can give and, without realizing it, we start a chain of sowing and harvesting, which starts from a seed of joy for both the giver and the receiver.

Let us note that when we give with a particular interest in mind, the real intention is not for the other person to benefit, but what we are going to receive in return. Hence, motivation loses focus on service. But when we are aware of what it means to give for the pleasure of serving and for the other person to receive the best of what is being given, then we will be opening the doors through which the reward, at the right time, will have to enter (even if we are not expecting it). It will come as a result of having sown with the only intention of making someone happy. Thus, another unbreakable universal principle is put into practice and we will be open to abundance. In the book **The Seven Spiritual Laws of Success** by Deepak Chopra he says: **"The Universe is a continuous flow that gives us what it receives"**.

Giving has to do with everything we can do for the benefit of others, whether it is something material, spiritual or emotional. A person who has learned the principle of giving is a person who will always experience abundance.

Releasing attachments and feelings of lack connects us to a life of prosperity. This means we are allowing the natural flow of abundance to manifest freely in us. It is opening our mind to the field of all possibilities for extraordinary things to happen in our life.

Finding purpose gives us the joy of waking up each day with enthusiasm, ready to enjoy only one day at a time, without thinking about yesterday or tomorrow; ready to see life through our spiritual eyes. Those that allow us to perceive the world in a different and positive way. Finding always open doors of blessing and opportunities for change. Having a life with purpose drives us to be better in everything we do, motivates us to look every day for new strategies to carry out our projects, makes our existence happy and connects us with the perfect vibration in the frequency of love.

If only today we decide to wake up with the mindset of making this day the best of our days, despite the inconveniences that may arise, we will certainly experience a special day and feel happy about this enriching earthly experience.

While it is true that much of something attracts more than it does, then the more we are ourselves, safe, transparent, with identity and character, allowing all our essence to flow from within, we will surely be opening the way to project our life towards constant growth and improvement that will lead us to enjoy happiness and success (remember that success is a personal result that does not depend on external approval).

The purpose, or what for, of our life, that reason why we came to this earthly plane, is within each of us waiting for us to discover it and project it. It is something that makes our existence happy and drives us to renew our way of thinking, to generate changes that will positively impact my life and my environment in general.

Finding the purpose of our life is a decision that challenges us, but at the same time motivates us. It is just wanting to find it and take the path that life itself is showing us.

It is very important that we keep in mind the difference between life purpose and projections, since the purpose has to do with the part of being and service. It is linked to the essence of each person. It is the reason for which I exist and this in turn allows me to enjoy full happiness.

But the projections are directed to the material and personal part. Of course, they also bring great joy to our lives, but these are momentary, while recognizing that they are part of the path to finding the purpose of our existence.

Living one day at a time frees us from the burden of thinking about the future and all that it implies. It empowers us to enjoy the present moment and thus be able to better manage our time, since from that morning we can program the day in a different way; not as a boring routine, but as a new opportunity that we can create ourselves. As we learn to live in the here and now, calm and confident in the knowledge that we have a focus, a life purpose that fills our days with joy and motivation; then we will know that the days from now on are destined for well-being, goal achievement and personal growth. It is from that moment on that our future begins to augur well founded success.

The purpose of our life is very much linked to living in the present time, with a calm mind and free of inoffensive thoughts so that in those moments of consciousness we can generate the encounter with your purpose. The purpose is sealed in your essence, it is like a mark of a special talent (which must have as an end, to be used for the benefit of you and others), and when you discover it, you understand that this is what fills your life with motivation, what makes you passionate, makes your blood boil, satisfies you and beautifies your life. In that encounter with that gift you can generously connect with love and happiness.

CHAPTER SIX
"Projections and goals"

All the objectives that someone has achieved in their life, whether big or small, came from a projection that had its beginning in a thought manifested through habits.

The most beautiful buildings, the means of transport, the technological innovations we enjoy today, entrepreneurs, professionals in all fields, marriages, travel, etc.; everything, absolutely everything originated first in someone's mind. It is in the mind where we begin to build our lives, but what comes out was produced by information that previously entered it. Just as our body reflects what we eat, so our way of thinking reflects what kind of food we have nourished the mind with. This is so real that we can see children wanting to imitate the superheroes on TV shows. They are guided by what is in their minds. This is the key point and I invite you to ask yourself the following questions (answer them for yourself): What kind of information am I feeding my mind? What kind of people do I spend most of my time with? What kind of reading am I doing? What kind of TV programs am I watching? What kind of places am I going to?

How many years have we been absorbing everything that is part of our environment, without stopping for a second to think if everything we see and hear provides us with constructive information that motivates us and encourages us to grow in order to access a better quality of life?

Simply as if we were non-thinking beings, we receive everything that comes to us without previously filtering it, knowing that this information could affect us later. Our brain is designed to store an amount of information that we cannot even imagine, but it does not differentiate between positive and negative, it simply retains everything. Our brain accumulates, and to that extent, all this information is what somehow shapes our life. This is as true as knowing that the culture of each place arises from a mindset. In other words, the accumulation of all the information that is inherited over time.

Let us observe that each region has its own customs. A lifestyle and way of doing things, a dialect, a specific accent, a dress style, a way of behaving and although all human beings are different, we cannot deny that each place has some characteristics that define it and in one way or another, these influence each person. All these behaviors that make up a culture have an origin and that origin is all the information that has been transmitted from generations to generations and that continues as an endless chain.

Each culture has its own idiosyncrasy, and what for one region may be considered good, for another may be taken as something bad. With this we confirm once again that we should not judge the behavior of others, since we ignore the manner in which they were raised.

We can find all kinds of customs, some of which may even be quite strange to those who were not trained under those same teachings. Every place is characterized by something special, whether it be its fauna, its folklore, its education, and so on. This has everything to do with the teaching that the community receives through what it hears and what it sees. Everything that is recorded in our brain was perceived consciously or unconsciously through our senses. Even the smallest details. Hence the importance of taking care of our language and attitudes towards our children, they should not in any way, even in jest, create fears, much less expose them to situations of mockery or shame. Children are always spoken to with the truth, they are motivated, empowered, and cared for in terms of what they hear and what they see, because their brain is constantly collecting everything it perceives from its environment. If a child is fearful from an early age, his or her self-confidence will be negatively affected. They will be afraid of being challenged, will not easily dare to speak in public or to undertake something new, will feel insecure when it comes to presenting a project, interviewing, or entering a relationship. Fortunately, in adulthood, with work and commitment, these kinds of patterns of behavior can be changed, but if you encourage confidence in the individual from childhood, you will certainly move faster on your path.

Starting from this fundamental point, *the mind*, we are now aware that we must begin by cleaning it and to do so the first thing will be to decide intelligently from here on in, what type of information we will allow into it. To all the things that motivate us, drive us, everything that instructs us to be better people, everything that makes us happy, fills us with peace and security; to everything that motivates us to dream, to share, to forgive, to heal the heart, to help others and to serve with love. It is to all this instruction that we will be attentive and ready to receive from now on. It is to all this new knowledge that we will open the doors of our mind until it becomes part of us and thus project us in a different way into the future.

Projections and goals are located on the same path. One is the complement of the other. They are the perfect combination. When a person projects in their mind, if they really long for something and decide to work for it, that projection becomes a goal. It is like when an athlete thinks about running a race and winning it, the first step is in his mind. The next one is when they project it, but if they don't prepare for that race, how can they win?

They must do everything in their power to achieve it. This means that perhaps while his friends are sleeping, they will need to get up earlier to train. They may be under great pressure and sometimes feel like giving up, but in the end, when the day comes, the result will be to reach the finish line. This is where the fruit of effort gains recognition.

I recommend that you watch the movie: Peaceful Warrior, in which you will be able to appreciate these concepts and strengthen them a little more.

Setting goals is less difficult than it seems, we could even say that we do it quite often. What we find difficult to maintain is the consistency and focus on achieving those goals. That is why when we fail to achieve a goal, we often feel frustrated and take on the role of victim.

Self-motivation sustains our momentum despite the obstacles. For this reason, we must understand that, if we work in projection with responsibility, we will achieve the goals we have set.

There are two words that we use so much on a daily basis that they have somehow lost the importance of their meaning. Not because they are no longer valuable, but because we utter them automatically. These words are **love** and **passion**. Without them, we will hardly reach the culmination of our objectives. We use them so unconsciously that in the end they have become something to which we do not give much meaning. That is why we need to take the time to rediscover the true meaning of them and discover all that we, human beings, can achieve. Acting consistently keeps us in alignment with our goals.

If we project in our mind something we want to achieve and start acting in coherence with that thought, the result will be to obtain what we have projected. Always focused on living in accordance with our way of thinking, without letting ourselves be distracted by the noise of the environment (developing a sense of intuition will allow us to identify what suits us). Bearing in mind that since previous chapters we have been in the process of practicing the art of cultivating the garden of thoughts, taking care of the information that we allow our senses to perceive.

When a person dreams, the Universe works in favor of their dreams. Whoever does not have dreams, only sees others get theirs. Sometimes we let the best years of our lives go by, only complaining about difficult situations, bad salaries, few opportunities, criticizing the country's policies, blaming our failures on anything that makes us feel better and less guilty, when the only ones responsible for our successes or failures is ourselves.

We all have capabilities, innate talents and great untapped potential. What happens is that sometimes we don't take the time to develop them to the fullest. Rather, we wait for others to do things for us, as it is easier for us to stay in the comfort zone.

Life is full of opportunities and they are abundant for everyone. It is up to each of us to project from our minds that life of fulfillment.

It's time to give up being one of those people who stay submerged in fleeting thoughts that come and go and in the end, nothing happens because they don't put their heart into their dream. Let's become part of those special beings who, decided with determination to armor our mind from now on and take care of it as the great treasure that it is. So that from now on, everything that is created inside it, will be big thoughts, projections that become goals and goals that become reality because we are always willing to give everything to achieve them.

There is a part of our mind that is the subconscious and we have the great responsibility of filtering what enters it. It absorbs all the information we receive and acts on its own according to it. The subconscious is like the earth that accepts any seed that is sown and fulfills its function of making it germinate. This explains why many times we, wanting to change certain behaviors and attitudes, do not succeed; since it is the subconscious that is acting according to the accumulation of images and information it has received. We can take control of our thoughts if we begin to consciously select what we see and hear. Certainly, it will take some time to detoxify the mind and that is why it is necessary to start here and now.

Empowering affirmations are a very useful tool for our minds to progress. Therefore, I invite you to strongly and decisively repeat these words and begin right now to plant seeds of greatness in your mind.

From now on I will not be left behind, watching others achieve their goals; I will not make excuses for anything or anyone for all that I have not achieved so far. From today on, I will look within myself, seek and find all the potential, all the talent and all the capabilities I have to achieve my dreams!

Assuming an attitude of commitment will not only motivate us to project our goals, but to put into action everything that brings us closer to the fulfillment of those objectives.

"Opportunities and gifts come to all those who adopt an attitude of fulfillment. This does not end or run out because the principles are inexhaustible." Mark Victor Hansen.

CHAPTER SEVEN
"Longing for life"

Life becomes peaceful for those of us who consciously choose to learn to live in the present tense, since we have usually been accustomed to living in terms of the past or the future, carrying guilt for something that happened or worrying about something that we don't even know if will ever happen.

Today is of immense value in itself, whether we possess material goods or not, of what has happened in the past or what will happen next. We cannot deny the importance of projecting and longing for beautiful moments that we hope to see come in our lives, but in no way can we stop being happy right now with what we have, because when that later comes, that happiness will be momentary; it will pass fleetingly and we will be starting another cycle of anxiety, hoping to be happy and complete only when we obtain what we need to feel in fullness.

This is our moment. The happiest day of our life is today. Today is the day to dream, to smile, to create, to make others happy, to be better at our job, to be better parents, better children, better friends, to say I love you, to do the work with excellence, to give a hug. Today is the day to get up early, to be on time for our appointments; and if for some reason you don't have a job, this is the best day to redirect your thoughts and believe that life is full of new opportunities. It is in difficult times when the imagination has to come alive, that we have to be sure that there are doors of new blessings waiting for us to open. Today is the day to learn to love life and enjoy it. Now is the right time to be grateful for everything we have and for everything life has given us throughout our existence. All human beings are born rich, since we possess a wonderful body equipped with the best functioning systems that nothing can equal. You can see this by the example of so many people who, even when lacking an organ in their body, have performed amazing feats in their lives.

Today is the day to think of all that is good, of all that brings happiness. To generate feelings of purity from our mind. Today is the perfect time to set goals for ourselves, to feed ourselves healthily, to dress with the best that we have kept for a long time in the closet waiting for the ideal occasion to come. Today is the best time to use your best perfume. Get ready to live this day as the best of all. Treat yourself to a special day today, feel beautiful or attractive, stand in front of the mirror and declare a word that exalts your values. Greet yourself with your best smile and leave your house with your head clear, full of good expectations. Only each of us can make the decision to make each day the most special of all. We are driven by an immense desire not to let another minute of our lives pass by because we have not become aware of this wonderful gift *"free will"*. That capacity and freedom that all human beings have to make decisions with responsibility. That which gives us the autonomy to do with our lives all that we desire, not in the sense of libertinism that leads to negative results of which we ourselves assume the consequences, but of that freedom that allows us to act in benefit of positive changes with which we will access a more prosperous and pleasant life. Freedom to respect myself and others, putting into practice the common sense that connects my well-being with that of the people around me.

It brings great personal satisfaction, to have other people grow with me. It's like a magnet that attracts fluidity and abundance to my own life. It is as if the doors are automatically opened for the field of all possibilities to unfold before us.

We often see people who have lost their desire to live and the worst thing is that they may not even have realized it, since they have become accustomed to seeing each day as the same old routine; routine, a word that we must begin to eliminate from our lexicon, since it prevents us from seeing each day as a new one, different from all others, regardless of whether it is sunny or rainy. Rather, I invite you to replace this word (routine) with all those that give us the power to predict a new and special day. It is a personal decision how we want to receive each morning. It is in our hands to make life a paradise. I would like to make a parenthesis to describe the word *"paradise"*, which refers to a peaceful and beautiful place/state. It is worth making this clarification because our mind has been so polluted and so removed from everything that really belongs to us, that some might think it is an illusion that such a place exists. You can paint the canvas of your life any way you want. You can paint a paradise, or you can simply paint a dark forest that causes you fear and anxiety. We are the ones who define the direction we want to take. We are the authors of our own history. It is we ourselves who open or close doors with our attitudes. We are the ones who make the decision to start every morning with all the courage and strength. It is us who prepare our hearts for the positive, for forgiveness, for optimism, for trust, faith and hope. It is us who motivate ourselves to be better. It is us who generate peace and tranquility in our environment. We are the

ones who make the change, who make the difference, who renew our minds every day, who decide to act in front of the circumstances and put an end to everything that prevents us from
being happy. We have in our hands the power to give life to our
life, the power to give a special touch to our existence. We can
soar like eagles and soar to the heights to see the immense panorama of opportunities for us and go for them. When an eagle
sees a storm coming, it rises and flies above it. So, we must
learn that when a difficult moment comes in our life it is when
we rise with positive thoughts and act with wisdom.

It is wise to flee from dangers. To keep a distance from
anything that could generate negative results in our life and
in the lives of others. It is also wise to choose well the people
with whom we spend most of our time, assuming an attitude of
commitment to ourselves in terms of our personal growth and
the care with which we constantly listen. I emphatically clarify
that it is not to set anyone aside, nor to think that there are better or worse people, but if we want to experience a better quality of life, we must take care of the whole environment with
which we surround ourselves without generating competition.

It is also wise to make good use of time. Learn to make decisions from the stage and not guided by our emotions. Learn
when it is a good time to talk and when it is better to be silent.
Knowing how to choose who to entrust with our personal affairs. These are the right behaviors that in the long run will
allow us to experience significant changes that will result in a
better and prosperous way of living.

Learning to listen to the voice of our heart (intuition) is
a good way to start making fewer mistakes. The voice of the
heart will always bring peace. When in a difficult or decisive

situation there is something which doesn't give you peace of mind or confidence, listen to this inner voice and let things flow without pressure. It is wise of us to take the time to listen to ourselves and to clear up our doubts.

Our path to an extraordinary life starts from that thought directed towards everything that somehow connects us to those states of tranquility of spirit, love, prosperity and everything that implies an abundant life in all areas, both emotional and material. These states are not limited to a certain space-time, but rather, are a state of the soul which is directly related to our inner being; which (states) we can experience in our daily life as something which remains stable within us and which is externalized through the usual events, but in a more harmonious and fluid way.

I hope with all my heart that this optimistic way of perceiving life will become inherent to all humans. Optimism to empower each one of us to think outside the box; to identify with that vision from here on out, until we make an impact on the world through clean and authentic thoughts.

Happiness is not a destination; it is not a place we will one day reach. It is a path that we choose to walk every day, regardless of what is happening around us. A person who achieves inner peace is definitely living in paradise. If we are calm and have peace, it is because we feel that everything is going well and there is nothing to worry about. It is not impossible; it is about learning to live on this earth by making it a heaven. Not because everything is as we expect it to be, but because we have learned to face each day, each circumstance however difficult it may seem, with courage and bravery. So much so, that nothing moves us from that position of tranquility. That even when the pressures arise, we are so prepared and aware of who we are, that they do not succeed in disrupting our inner peace.

"The essence of existence consists in the capacity of the human being to respond responsibly to the demands that life places on him, in each particular situation." -Viktor Frankl

At this point, it is useful to mention the diseases with which we are familiar today; one of the most common ones is the stress caused by the worry and anxiety in which most people live. This common illness, which like all others, comes from the soul (the soul is the seat of emotions). Our emotional side directly affects our body health. A person who has no control over his or her emotions is much more vulnerable to stress. This has become so natural, that it is already part of everyday expressions, to the point of being expressed without reason, continuously and automatically at any time throughout our day. We have become accustomed to constantly repeating this expression, that we ourselves have given it the strength to become one of the diseases of the century and have transformed it into a reality within our lives.

The statement "I'm stressed out" is another one of those disempowering statements that we must eliminate from our vocabulary, as we mentioned before. What I speak of, that's what my mind is full of; it's as simple as that. As I think and act, that's what I make of my own existence. So, let us begin today to eliminate from our lexicon the word stress, because that word produces in us anxiety, instability, eagerness and consequently, makes our body sick. This is a reality which we can only face by remaining attentive, and not thinking about that word again, and if we do think about it, immediately replacing it with an opposite phrase like *"I am calm."* I can assure you that in a few minutes you will begin to experience changes and calm attitudes in your behavior.

Every time we think of everything that attracts us to wellness, positive energies, fun, good health, we are self-motivating, and all these positive thoughts produce healthy emotions. It is an intelligent way to learn to live, to make our daily life a continuous source of joy. Truly, life becomes more beautiful when we renew our perception of it. Not because everything is rosy, but because we are giving ourselves the task of changing, of daring to be uncomplicated, calm and respectful of others' thoughts and lifestyles. You may wonder why throughout the book the mindset and actions of others are mentioned repeatedly and the answer is, because everything that affects us positively or negatively has to do with the environment and the people around us. (Think about it: couples, ex-partners, children's or our children's teachers, friends, children, parents, co-workers or fellow students, neighbors, drivers, etc.) There are always people connected to what we think and feel.

Life is transformed when our environment no longer strongly affects us in our ability to assume it. That is, whether the environment is pleasant or unpleasant, our attitude remains calm. In such a way that we face each moment with sensibility up to the point of being able to convert those situations that seemed unfavorable, into passing moments from which we manage to emerge out of with a good teaching that edifies us and encourages us to continue with the certainty that everything has a special purpose to benefit us.

Life is so beautiful that, if we could at least see it clearly in our minds, we would not waste the slightest opportunity to give our best without any qualms, without looking at whether other people deserve it or not. Without thinking about how much we are giving and how little we are receiving, but rather we will be willing to give a little more until we spread to others all the good that we have inside and become part of the change that we want to see in our society.

We already know that we should not wait for anyone to change, but that we are who is beginning to renew their mind and as a consequence of this, changes in our environment are beginning to emerge. My transformation is rewarded or reflected with positive changes in people in whom I hope to see better attitudes. This is a chain that can be lengthened increasingly.

When I externalize what has virtue, such as kindness, respect, loyalty, transparency, a good sense of humor, silence instead of offense, everything that produces a healthy coexistence, all this comes back multiplied in blessings in all areas of my life.

Our body reveals what we are on the inside. The healthier my soul is, the healthier my body is. The more inner harmony I experience, the more harmonious my body will be. That's how magical the way this works is. You can only see it if you believe it and put it into practice, it's a matter of decision. You can start today. This is the best day to believe in yourself and trust others. It is the best time to start seeing in the people around you all the virtues and values they have.

Bring out your talents on this day. If you can play a musical instrument, play it and enjoy it to the fullest. If you are an artist or even if you think you are not, dare to paint a picture, sing a song, write a poem, send a letter to a loved one, give a flower. Make as many people as you can happy, starting with yourself. Fix your hair, give yourself a compliment, prepare a good meal and invite someone over to share with you. Forgive those who have offended you and forget these events, it is the best way to heal yourself. Throw away resentment in a place where you won't find it again, how about in the past? -This one will never come back, unless you go looking for it. Strive to be yourself every day, but in an improved version. Take care of your mental and physical health, get some exercise, go for a walk. Admire and feel nature, take a bath in a river, go somewhere beautiful. Make today an exceptional day, you will see that it is easy to replace the negative with the positive. If you manage to make today the best day, without anything extraordinary having to happen other than what you decide to create yourself, then you will have found the secret that will allow you to enjoy plenitude.

If you find yourself in an unfavorable situation, if you see the doors of opportunity closed, if you feel weakened by the pressures you are facing, and even if you have lost the motivation to live, *I challenge you to make one more attempt.* I dare you to be brave, to stand in front of the mirror and ask yourself, looking into your eyes: Am I a loser? -And if deep in your heart you feel that you are not and, this is most certainly what will happen because the Source will confirm it to you, look into your eyes again and with strength from the depths of your being, declare this: *I was born to succeed. I can successfully accomplish anything I set my mind to. I am skilled and capable. I have the potential to succeed. I am brave and can face the challenges that life presents. I believe in myself. I can forgive and free myself from the past. I can set goals for myself and achieve them. I have the ability to dig deep within myself until I discover who I really am. I am the perfect love. I am spiritual essence!*

The statements incite the Universe to work on your behalf. They open your mind with new thoughts and bring emotional balance, as well as lead you to trust more in yourself and in that unconditional help from the Universal Source. You can include this practice every time you look in the mirror (preferably in the morning and before you go to sleep). Remind yourself how valuable you are and how much you can achieve. Take this opportunity to say a kind word to yourself. There are many expressions that we can say to ourselves, use your creativity. Just as we've heard that plants become lusher when spoken to with love, so do we.

The desire not only to survive but to live happily and fully has everything to do with the coherence between what we think and what we say. I encourage you to risk reinventing yourself every day in different ways, allowing yourself to enjoy an extraordinary life without limitations.

CHAPTER EIGHT
"Building a New World"

In spite of seeing and hearing about violence, theft, suicide, divorce, hatred, war, drugs, prostitution and so many other situations that are affecting the world through the media or in daily conversations, we cannot deny that we like to live quietly, comfortably, safely and enjoying high-quality of life; although at the same time we see it as something difficult to achieve considering the reality that is lived in today's world. However, some of us think that it is possible to live in a better world. There are people who believe that by starting with ourselves we can motivate change in many and these changes could be transmitted to many more. To think this way is not a utopia, is to live with the faith that this can be a reality, because the same amount of energy we use to think negative thoughts, is what we could use to think positive thoughts. The best way to start is by believing that we can improve our surroundings, that small circle of family, friends, neighbors, co-workers or colleagues and those people we meet in our daily lives. We can do this by using simple but powerful strategies. For example, good attitudes, behaviors that seek a healthy coexistence, respect, simplicity, collaboration, even understanding. Learning to cultivate the art of overlooking the mistakes of others, just as we would like them to overlook any mistakes we make. Sometimes we give too much importance to the words or attitudes coming from people who offend us, I say in quotation marks because nobody really offends us, we are the ones who decide to perceive it that way. Here it is worth highlighting the confidence in oneself, knowing that I am what I am regardless of what others think or say. When a person is sure of themselves, they know who they are and what they are worth, whether other people recognize them or not.

"When you judge others you don't define them, but you define yourself as someone who wants to judge." - Wayne W. Dyer.

Learning to master the ego and control emotions, simply being ourselves frees us from heavy burdens and leads us to much clearer and simpler paths. We possess many important values that facilitate our life experience here on earth. Most people long for a peaceful world, but we almost always look for it on the outside without realizing that it is within ourselves where it really lies. *"I, myself, create peace from my own thoughts, words and attitudes"*.

There are many ways to generate peace. For example, when we understand that we can say things without having to raise our voice. That a loving look can heal a resentful heart. That extending a hand to help another person makes many hands reach out to help in a time of need. To cultivate the habit of being a tidy person, something that might seem irrelevant or not worth mentioning here, but I can assure you that a clean and tidy environment generates peace of mind. A person who is impeccable with their personal appearance, tidy with the management of their finances, with their housework and their workplace. A person who always arrives on time for their appointments. An orderly person that commits himself only to the commitments they can fulfill. A person who is well-balanced with his or her expenses. This type of person transmits to others credibility and confidence. This process of order in the different areas of our life results in prosperity and joy.

Life is made of moments, each one of them is a new opportunity for growth and the best thing of all is that we have in our hands the capacity to take all the good things from them and continue learning.

Sometimes we are faced with criticism or negative attitudes in which it would be good for us before getting angry, to observe our thoughts and try to see in those criticisms a possibility to recognize our faults and improve, or perhaps simply to see that they are only words and that they do not change the essence of what we are. My essence remains unchanged by external factors unless I allow them to affect me. The important thing in life's journey is not to stop and struggle with every obstacle that comes our way, but to learn to face them and find a solution, because there is always at least one.

We must recognize that there are people with better skills, with more experience and with a broader knowledge that are steps ahead of us, but this cannot be an excuse to stop, feel bad or think that we are inferior to them; on the contrary, it does us a lot of good to encounter those kinds of people along the way, to follow and learn from. People who inspire admiration in us. We should always look at others as our teachers because we learn something from them. The Universe is wide and always connects us with that which brings us closer to our goals.

It is inspiring to see that there are things which are much easier to achieve with a smile than with the use of force. Valuing principles and practicing good habits definitely attunes us to the higher vibrations of happiness.

My invitation is to reconnect with the true meaning of life. Be consistent with our actions, with common sense. The one that says, "*I do to others what I would like them to do to me*".

Respect for children is essential. Love them and educate them because they are our successors. Generating moments of quality to share with them, stimulating their creativity, strengthening their personal security, allowing them to be happy, directing them to dream and being committed to their dreams, are ways of connecting with the meaning of our lives.

The place where the foundations of society are found and where good habits should be encouraged is in our own home. Everything that children perceive within their home is what will largely be directing their behaviors and attitudes when they are the men and women of tomorrow.

Let us consider the idea of being autonomous in our way of thinking, taking advantage of that capacity we have to act out of our own conviction, in order to transform our life into a successful one as a result of the decisive decisions we make.

To give value to the word, to fulfill what we promise, to tell the truth, are valuable principles that influence very positively in that transformation. Stay as far away as possible from criticism (negative energies that keep us from a prosperous life). If possible, have a compassionate attitude towards those people who, by their words or actions, show their lack of meaning and love for life. It is better to seek harmony rather than to pretend to be right; it is better to breathe deeply and be silent, than to attack others with our words and perhaps later have to repent.

Whenever possible, let us become part of the solution. Everything we do and express comes back to us multiplied by universal law, so let's do as much good as possible.

To start creating our own real world, free of any negative feelings or thoughts, it is necessary to stop giving life to the past, it is the best formula to transform the present. Freeing yourself from any kind of disempowering thought clears the mind. Those memories only achieve to exhaust our neurons unnecessarily thinking about a past that separates us from reality. It is here and now that I decide how I think, how I speak and how I act. Life takes on a very special meaning when we begin to live in the present tense, since each moment is unique and will never be repeated in the same way again. Every moment has its importance and value, understanding that we are the ones who bring color and joy to them. We could start by giving it the valuable meaning that the moment has when we sit down to eat, it is one of the best moments of the day. Are we enjoying it as it should be? Or, on the contrary, is our mind so absent that we overlook the tastes, smells, colors, shapes and something as fundamental as the gratitude for the daily provision? Something daily and simple, but at the same time valuable and confronting, because what would happen if we didn't have it?

The new world begins within me. A world that surfaces to be part of change; change that begins in my thoughts.

Every human being is a world within themselves. It is different from others, but at the same time it is part of a whole and as such, it affects it. Each one has the capacity to choose how they want to see and perceive their world, as well as to transform it into something better if they so choose.

Each of us decides how we want to create our world. A real world where we have the possibility to choose everything, we want it to contain. Each one of us chooses which colors to paint our days with and how much joy to inject into our lives. Each person has in his hands the power to transform his world into a colorful, joyful, passionate, prosperous, calm, abundant and happy place.

If you wish, you can make your life so transparent that it can be seen through your eyes. You can make those who come to you absorb from that source of good things within you. Wherever you arrive, you can harmonize with your presence and wherever you go, you can leave traces of joy. You can, if you wish, make your life so radiant that it illuminates everything around you and that your reflection is that of a person who, although he or she may be mistaken, is constantly improving; that although he or she may be talented and daring, he or she always maintains his or her simplicity; that although he or she has money in his or her pocket, has achieved his or her goals and is successful, he or she continues to be humble.

Regardless of race or skin color, economic status or any other type of differential barrier imposed by the system, we all emerge from the same source. We are all endowed with the same capabilities and have the same opportunities to achieve our goals as we project them in our minds. *"The only limitation of the human being is their own mind"*.

Thought produces an emotion that materializes through the force that we ourselves give it and the Universe will work in favor of that vision. For this reason, the more I nourish myself with positive information, that's what my life is becoming. What I put in my mind generates thoughts and emotions.

Just simply listen to a person speak, to know the kind of information they have in their head; depending on what they say, that is how their inner self is and therefore how they live. I allow myself to redound to the same concepts, because it is the way to see radical changes not only in our life but also in our environment, *taking care of the garden of our thoughts*. And to think better, I must inevitably have a wider expectation that what I see and hear must always be focused on everything that leads me to a more optimistic perspective on life.

This is a way of being coherent; simply the state of my life reflects the state of my mind.

Speaking positively must be accompanied by an optimistic and joyful attitude towards life, because that feeling that everything is fine will produce a vibration so powerful that it will make the thought materialize faster.

A new world includes principles and values in a special way, since they are like a platform that drives us to grow in all areas; practicing humility, honesty, loyalty, responsibility, respect, are some of the virtues that position a human being in higher vibrational levels. Which, indeed, will result in prosperity in all areas and personal satisfaction as remuneration.

If in the morning you decide to undertake not only another day but an excellent day, with the mind set on the fact that you will encounter some difficulty along the way, if you maintain your best attitude and make use of your free will to decide how to assume it with the greatest show of elevated thoughts toward yourself and others, then you will have as a result at the end of the day, the great satisfaction of seeing yourself as a winner. Maybe not better than other people, but better than who you were yesterday. You will realize there is no obstacle you cannot overcome, and those obstacles only make you stronger, faster, firmer and more decisive in achieving your goals. All this will give you the motivation to project yourself again every morning and to turn your life into a constant source of joy and triumph. You will begin to perceive difficulties as opportunities for growth and thus be able to experience yourself in different ways.

Those who decide to give up and fall behind in their helplessness and sadness should know that the world goes on and that it does not feel sorry for anyone. Time will continue to move forward every day with giant steps and every wasted moment is life that is no longer enjoyed and knowledge that is no longer acquired.

Words are a special power we possess. Everything we speak takes shape and strength. It is very convenient to practice the conscious use of words, not to speak for the sake of speaking, but to try to be aware of the scope of our expressions, since with them we give life to pleasant or unpleasant circumstances. With our words we build, heal and forgive. With words we communicate and at the same time we generate changes. A sweet word can break down strong walls of intolerance and hate. It can heal a wounded heart and even save a relationship that is about to end. A loving word can change a person's life in an unimaginable way.

"Guard my mouth, guard the door of my lips." Psalm 141:3 RVR1960

Every word that comes out of our mouth produces an echo in the Universe that always returns and when it does, it does so with more force.

Words are creative. If you talk about a person, these words create more of the same in them. So do you. So if you expect to see different results in a person or a circumstance, but you're always talking about how bad it is, the incorrect way they do things or how badly they treat you, you will continue to get more of what bothers you.

Whatever the situation we are facing at some point, talking about the negatives will not solve anything. Although sometimes it can be difficult not to express the non-conformity we are experiencing at the moment, I assure you that it is possible to contain ourselves and obtain different results.

Life is a constant source of moments that offer us the opportunity to bring out our essence, to bring out those behaviors that reveal who we really are. A person can refer to themselves or to others in a particular way, but it is the behaviors that reveal the truth.

There are people who explode with anger and can even reach the point of physically attacking someone; as we also see those who just by looking express affection, smile, give thanks and in the face of an adverse moment, assume a serene attitude. There are peacemakers who, with an attitude of humility, manage to placate the anger of others. They are different expressions and each one of them is a reflection of what people keep inside. Many times, a hug has given someone the strength to stand up and move on. Many dialogues have managed to suspend great conflicts. Wars can be stopped with a gesture of humility. This does not mean that when we are humble, we lose dignity or respect; on the contrary, being humble makes us great, strengthens our character and positions us in a state of freedom. Humility frees us from prejudice. The more inner peace we have, the more peace we have outside.

Each person has countless people in their environment and each of us is an essential part of an endless chain of vibrations. Transmitting good to others allows us to enjoy everything the universe gives us in return. *Stimulating and motivating* people who are part of our environment, children, parents, siblings, friends, co-workers, employees or even someone we barely know, is a powerful practice that produces very positive changes very noticeable and immediate.

Motivation is that spark that drives us to carry out a certain action with enthusiasm. It is that force that makes us want to achieve a certain goal. When a person is motivated, they have a greater impulse to achieve their dreams. Motivation brings with it joy, faith, strength, decision and commitment. It allows us to feel alive and makes us see in every adverse situation, an opportunity to take out all the potential we have inside, to put it to the test.

We can all begin to build our new world with a perspective of our own, one that makes it easier for us to see beyond what was previously impossible to visualize. An optimistic and happy perspective aimed at positively impacting your environment and therefore society.

All the new habits that we start to include from now on in our daily practices will have a significant impact on the results that we will obtain from now on. Building a new world is nothing more than having your life your own way. It is nothing more than projecting in your mind the life you want to have and focusing on it by leaning on these concepts we have shared. Put a blank page in your mind and consciously decide what you want to put on it from now on. It's your life, it's your time, it's your dreams, it's your canvas. There are no excuses, no limitations, just a sea of new opportunities to be explored and a wide road to be traveled. It is not the current politician, it is not the lack of money, it is not the system, it is not the humble family you may belong to, *it is your decision* to be decisive and committed to your goals and dreams. *Simply, you are the writer and protagonist of your own story.*

CHAPTER NINE
"Silence and Wisdom"

It is not so common to find people who like to listen, usually most people feel more comfortable talking. Talking is a wonderful way to communicate and if you think about it carefully, you will find that there is a lot to explore about this topic that is perhaps simple, but at the same time, complex.

Every day we share with people, listen to conversations of all kinds and according to the way they express themselves verbally we get an idea of their personality. There are people who can talk for long periods of time. A lecturer will speak according to the knowledge he or she has about the topic he or she is speaking about. A couple in love perhaps about their relationship and their projects. Friends and partners when they meet, talk about their personal and business affairs. Sometimes we meet people who exhaust us with too much talk, those who raise their voices, who strongly assault us with their words and even cause wounds in our hearts. Often, we also encounter beautiful words of strength and love that manage to lift our spirits; words that cheer us up and motivate us to live.

Words have the power to give life, but they can also take it away. This concept may seem strong, but it is a reality. Sometimes an unwelcome word can trigger unnecessary conflict.

In silence we listen to our inner voice. That voice that speaks to us from our essence and that we almost never listen to because we remain wrapped in the mental noise that produces anxiety.

In silence the thought is cleared. In deep, conscious breathing, our brain is oxygenated. New ideas come to our mind and creativity flows more easily. In silence our soul finds rest and connects again with the creative source.

However, we must know the difference between silence out of fear and silence out of knowledge. For when we are silent out of fear we deny ourselves the opportunity to express what we feel, we show insecurity, we give up being authentic, we stop giving other people ideas that can be useful to them and we deprive ourselves of the opportunity to radiate our light to others.

Instead, silence for knowledge elevates us to a higher level of thinking. It is only in the silence, in the intimacy of my inner self, that I can hear the voice of my heart telling me who I am, where I come from and where I am going.

Not everyone knows or has ever asked: who am I? If we asked ourselves this question right now, what would we answer? What would be the definition of myself?

Take a few minutes to do the exercise and you will realize how much or how little you know yourself. Keep in mind for your answers that not our jobs, age, or social position really define us as the fundamental beings that we are.

In silence we learn to use our intuition. By connecting with ourselves we access the resources we possess as extensions of the Universe that we are. Within us are power, willpower, love, compassion, truth, creativity, security and happiness. This is why we must seek these gifts within ourselves and activate them so that we can then radiate them to others.

By being silent and listening to our inner voice, we can acquire answers to solve any situation, since we develop the intelligence to make our senses more attentive and receptive, as well as learn to focus our strengths towards a defined objective, since we know we have enough power to dominate over emotions and the capacity to take the best advantage of adversities.

Every person has the intrinsic ability to master and transform their weaknesses into strengths, which allow them to enjoy a more abundant and fuller life, only many have not yet discovered this.

Developing introspection motivates us to grow as people. It connects us with our essence and helps us to improve our relationship with the environment in which we live. Not knowing ourselves leaves us vulnerable to any situation, however small it may seem.

"The greatest wisdom in existence is to know oneself". Galileo Galilei

We can resort to silence to connect with the Higher Self or Creative Mind, to give a break to our earthly pursuits that so much distract us from our natural state of tranquility and balance. We can also use silence to give ourselves time to breathe deeply and feel our heart beating. This vital organ that we rarely think about and which is rarely thanked for doing its job perfectly and in sync.

Silence allows us to connect with our senses. We learn to give importance to every cell in our miraculous body and we also learn to give ourselves quality time. There is something profoundly special and magical in silence (meditation) and that is the development of the sixth sense as Napoleon Hill says in his book "Think and Get Rich":

"The sixth sense is the portion of the subconscious mind: the creative imagination." Which allows us to commune with God or The Universal Mind, depending on your belief.

In the hustle and bustle of everyday life, we forget everything about ourselves. We become disconnected from purpose. We don't know who we are or where we are going, we just walk in the same direction that others are going.

Silence provides us with tools that help us stay focused on the improvement of our own lives. In silence we can meditate on our existence, the way we have been evolving our minds, the decisions we have made and the results they have brought to our lives. In silence we become aware of the present time, here where we are sowing the seeds that will bloom tomorrow. Seeds that may be of abundance, health, joy and prosperity, but which in their absence may also be of sadness and disappointment if we do not take care of the gift that life is giving us now.

In silence we learn to enjoy the company of ourselves. Many people are afraid of loneliness and have not realized that in loneliness we can strengthen our self-esteem, since we have the time to devote to our personal growth to empower ourselves and acquire new knowledge that we can later share with someone else.

Having moments of solitude is a necessary experience that can be completely enriching and healthy for any human being. The positive results that silence causes are more powerful than we might think, as it increases creativity and improves our mental and physical health.

Unfortunately, sometimes we miss this benefit because of the fear of feeling abandoned by others and this does not mean that we do not enjoy the presence of other people who also bring valuable experiences to our lives, but the point here is to give ourselves the task of discovering who we really are; thus giving us small moments of silence and stillness, to start listening to the sound of our inner voice. That voice that performs the function of connecting us with that which makes us feel confident, happy and at peace.

We do not have to stop living or sharing with others, just learn to enjoy those short spaces of restoration and personal attention.

In the silence of our home we cultivate the freedom to be ourselves without prejudice. We can show ourselves as we are without masks. *It is our encounter with authenticity, which is a virtue that refers to what I am, think and do when no one sees me.* If as the human beings we are, with successes and failures, we accept with love all that we are, not having a reason to hide from anyone and being able to assume our life with transparency, it is there where we begin to be truly free from thought. This authenticity will allow us to reach the limit of our self-confidence, since being as we want to be will not depend on what other people think or expect of us, but on what each one of us decides to be and do on our own initiative.

An authentic person goes outside the methods and traditions; they explore by their own means different ways of living and doing things. They create their own inner revolution.

An authentic person is happier because they are definitely what they want to be. They step outside the parameters imposed by a society influenced by egos and vanity (defining the ego as that pattern of thinking that binds us to live by comparing ourselves with others. This leads us to believe that we are superior or inferior to other people. Which makes us feel offended. Which makes us want to be right. Which separates us from the essence) and instead, gives us the opportunity to discover in our inner world everything that allows us to have a healthy and bias-free mentality.

Each one of us, regardless of race, sex, all without exception, possess an abundant inner world full of strength, of wonderful creative ideas that from love await an awakening that allows them to manifest through us.

We can conclude this chapter by recognizing the connection that exists between silence and wisdom; since everything that has wisdom emerges from that perfect and constant connection with intuition and the heart. They are your guides and your compass, which direct the course of your life towards a happy and promising horizon.

Wisdom is within you, it is part of your being, it is the sensuality and prudence with which you assume every circumstance of your existence. It is what leads you morally on the right paths to your growth. This wisdom is not a secret, nor is it hidden, it only awaits you in the silence and peace of your heart.

In this process of acquiring the habit of enjoying the silence to know ourselves, we become more sensitive to hear that voice whispering in our ear who we are and all that we could achieve if we believe it is possible.

The invitation is to make the decision to be you, to be authentic.

Accept yourself, with your height, your hair or skin color, with your successes and your failures, with your past. Accept that you are valuable. Accept yourself and love yourself. Enjoy the process of your evolution and remember that for a butterfly to have wings with beautiful colors, it first had to go through a transformation.

Silence and wisdom go hand-in-hand...

CHAPTER TEN
"Foundation of my life"

Foundation: principle or basis.

Let's take a moment to ask ourselves two questions that will help us discover the quality of foundation on which our life has been founded and in turn can serve as a guide to determine whether the foundations on which we are projecting our future will allow us to make our future promising.

1. According to the life you have now, what is the quality of your principles?

2. What is the quality of the foundation you are using to build your future?

Take a few minutes to think and answer honestly so that you will have a clearer focus as you read this chapter. If you prefer, write down your answers on a piece of paper and at the end of the chapter you will have a good starting point to begin reviewing the foundation of your life and will also be offered some guidelines to help you move forward in your personal growth.

Every person is a miraculous creation. If we remember in the beginning of the book we were commenting on the process of gestation in the mother's womb, in which our earthly existence begins its development. We know that from the moment of conception a being begins to exist that will gradually be formed, it is the beginning of a life within another life. The progenitor assumes a position of responsibility and care for this new being and the quality of the principles that they put into it, will depend largely on the way in which this new person will assume each circumstance during the course of their life.

Let us think of a woman who is in the process of gestation; we know that the baby is receiving all the information from the environment through its mother. The fetus perceives everything that is happening outside, and all this becomes part of it. These are the first foundations, but they will later have an impact on that person even in his or her adulthood.

It should be clarified that the fact that a person finds happiness and is successful, does not depend only on what he received or did not receive in his childhood, it will depend on how they assume their decision to change in the present as a first step to achieve it.

On this subject of children, both for those who are experiencing it now and for those who plan to do so later, it is interesting to get some training on what a mother's words, attitudes, moods and emotions influence in the formation of her child's security and character. I am referring to the mother, since she is the direct transmitting source towards this being in gestation, although the father and the environment also influence both the pregnant woman and the child. After the birth of this new being, the foundation process continues based on everything the child sees and hears in its environment. *We can call this accumulation of words and behaviors, which will produce positive or negative emotions, a foundation or principle.*

Each event within the home is an image that the child's mind records and turns into a guideline that tells them that this is the right way to solve the situations that arise in their daily lives. These events generate security or insecurity and a series of manifestations which define the personality of the child who will later become an adult. The lifestyle of the parents and the child's environment will be like their life manual from then on. By understanding this part of the foundations of every human being, we can be more aware that it is a chain of teachings that begins in childhood and continues throughout our lives, since we are always in constant evolution.

Motivation and empowerment in children are an excellent preparation for enjoying a well-structured life tomorrow, which will surely be much more peaceful and fulfilling. It is like a construction, everything is of vital importance in the process, from the plans to the completion of the project. It is necessary to have solid foundations to build reliable and safe buildings.

If we think in this way about something that is of a material nature, we must give greater importance to the formation of human beings, using solid foundations that help us to remain firm in the face of any difficulties encountered along the way of our existence.

Let us evaluate our personal foundations, regardless of our age, whether we are married or single, whether we have children or not; let us investigate within ourselves and observe the kind of behavior we assume in the face of each situation that presents itself to us daily. Let's put all these attitudes in a balance and with honesty let's provoke change in those areas where we have shortcomings and need improvement.

In no way should we excuse our failures in the way our parents taught us or the environment in which we grew up. On the contrary, it is our duty to recognize that we have in our hands the master key that opens all the doors that lead to our dreams and that we only need to assume a position of change. Forgiveness, honesty, gratitude, and determination are virtues that all human beings are capable of developing and the only thing we require is to have initiative of our own.

We can definitely, if we want to, have the determination to change all those old patterns of behavior that have been directing our reactions to certain circumstances in a negative way. For example, if someone offends us, the usual thing would be to react negatively to that attitude (this would be an old pattern of behavior). That is where I can make use of intelligence and free will, where without pressure from anything or anyone, I can decide to change that old foundation. That information I acquired in previous events, possibly in childhood, but that does not have to be my life manual in the present.

Now I am aware that I can know myself, identify my weaknesses to turn them into strengths, take control of my thoughts, words, and attitudes, and give them a new focus to drive my personal growth.

No negative attitude from anyone towards us should hurt us, condition our reaction, much less mark our destiny, but it depends on the firmness of our foundation whether they do or don't. Each person acts according to their level of consciousness, and those people who attack others do so because they are not aware that there are a number of different attitudes that could give them a higher mental capacity. It is worth mentioning here to implement the foundation of extended compassion towards those who sometimes react negatively.

If I decide today to lay a foundation of quality within myself, I will become an inspiring person. These foundations will promote us to be better parents, spouses, friends, bosses, employees, or whatever role we play in this society. The principles of quality add values and virtues in a human being, giving him/her the opportunity to reach higher levels of security and personal development.

This is the best time to lay the foundations of loyalty in everything we undertake from here on out. Foundations that will make us people who can be trusted. It is time to tear down those obsolete foundations that have kept us in the anonymity of our own lives; ideologies that subjected us for so long to mental illness, depressions, and unnecessary anguish. We now have in our hands the opportunity to make decisions for change that will lead us to explore a different dimension of joy, inner peace, and prosperity.

Today is the day to start acting differently and achieve our ideals. Today is the day to tear down that old foundation of procrastination and launch ourselves into believing that our life doesn't have to be the same, no matter if it has been good or not, we can simply transform it into a much better life.

Let's take control of our thoughts and focus them on change. Well-being is not just for a few; everything that others have achieved, we can achieve as well. There is nothing impossible for a mind that generates thoughts of greatness.

Let's take the risk of finding within ourselves the security and everything that raises our self-esteem. It is possible to live a peaceful and happy life. Every moment of our existence is a moment of decision; that is why I invite you to get up every morning with a word of thanks for the new day, with a smile of fulfillment, with the burning desire to be better than the day before and with the courage to face all your fears and realize what you are capable of doing. With the decision to throw yourself into doing everything that makes you happy, to work with love and make the most of every second of the gift of your life. Decide to commit to your goals and dreams. Watch less TV and read more books that will bring growth to your life. Play sports, go running in your neighborhood. Dare to learn how to play a musical instrument or do something you've always wanted to do, like studying for a job or starting your own business. Talk to a stranger, be creative. Dare to eat a food you've never tasted before. It's time to act. The decision to change brings powerful results that you can experience for yourself; you can start with small things that will surely motivate you to continue with bigger things that will lead you to enjoy and live life in an amazing way.

Changes, like stay away from criticism. Bless and forgive those who have acted in ways that displease us, implement good treatment at home, write down your goals and purposes in a notebook; it is these small changes that produce great transformations.

Don't expect others to do what you think or expect of them in order to accept them and feel happy. Decide to take responsibility for your defeats or momentary failures without blaming anyone, not even yourself; just accept them as a valuable part of progress and strength for your life.

Let us implore our hearts to be useful and helpful. Let's find a way back to civility, to those standards of good manners, education and respect for others that create quality relationships. Let us decide to replace all old inner talk of sickness and old age with all that contains health and longevity. Remember that you have within you the power to master your thoughts and emotions, keep them in balance. No longer are you fluctuating between intermittent moods that keep you anchored in one point. *Develop willpower.* Of course you can do it!

I invite you to declare these words and to feel them deep in your heart:

"Today I, *your name*, choose from this day forward to see all my days in the same shade of the color of hope. From this moment on, I consciously take control of my thoughts. I decide that no adversity will have the power to change my empowering attitude towards life and I will delight in the wonderful gift of being able to decide and be decisive in achieving my dreams. Today I decide to implant in me the feeling of gratitude for the gift of health that keeps me alive and for all that has always been supporting me in my earthly life experience. Thank you, Source, because I can smile, love, and be happy."

The way I act perfectly reflects the way I think. My actions are one hundred percent the fruit of my thoughts. The same situation can be handled in different ways, depending on each person's mindset, and results emerge accordingly. For this reason it is good to highlight the very constructive and harmonious effects that free us from the foolish thought of wanting to be right, because at this point we consciously know that each person believes that he or she has the truth and in addition to this, there is the truth as such. That is, there will always be three truths: your truth, my truth, and the truth as such. Who is right? - This is not what really matters, because *"It is better to be at peace than to pretend to be right."*

Listening to others without prejudice is a healthy way to learn to respect other people's thoughts without getting into disputes. Each person thinks and assumes life in a different way that is neither correct nor incorrect, it is just different; since we are all thinking beings endowed with intelligence and talents, which allow us to evolve through the free expression of our thoughts and motivations.

Having our lives founded on solid foundations helps us to resolve situations in an assertive manner, promoting us towards the achievement of increasingly significant objectives. Some people will say that they are not interested in achieving great feats, that perhaps they just want to enjoy life and be happy, but it all depends on the meaning that these people give to the feeling of happiness and it is totally respectable.

An example of transformation is given by nature itself, as is the process of the caterpillar becoming a butterfly. She gives way to the greatest transition of her life inside the chrysalis she has created with her own effort. After this transformation, she will emerge as a beautiful butterfly. In the same way, a person can make many mistakes and can find themselves in a difficult situation, such as depression, lack of motivation for life, an economic or love crisis; situations that we human beings go through in our daily lives and that sometimes we don't know how to face up to in the right way, depending on the initiative and determination of each one of us, remaining submerged in hardship or advancing with courage to discover the exceptional things waiting for us.

All adverse situations, some more difficult than others, but in the end difficult for those who are experiencing them, can be transformed. We can learn to take control of those situations that we think have gotten out of hand. Whatever the difficulty, there is a solution. Even the most delicate illness or the most critical economic situation has one or several solutions. The principle is to try to release the thought of helplessness, suffering and pain and then begin to trust that there is a way in the Universe to resolve that situation. It is to give that ray of light of hope a chance to enter through the window of our mind.

An easy way to start would be to replace all thoughts of sadness, suffering, weakness and anxiety with thoughts of faith. Faith is maintaining the firm confidence that something our physical eyes do not yet see can become real. The power of faith allows us to experience true miracles at any time in our lives, but faith alone does not produce results, it is not enough to say "I have faith or I believe"; it requires action and projection so that through it (faith) things will materialize.

"Faith is the eternal elixir that gives life, power and action to the impulse of thought." - Napoleon Hill

"It is therefore faith that is the certainty of things hoped for and the conviction of things not seen." Hebrews 11:1 ESV

Faith produces a sense of security. When a person desires something with passion, it can be material or emotional, and inside they believe they can get it, that security that they will have it generates peace of mind and joy; but if on the other hand we yearn for something, whatever it is, and see it as something impossible to realize, that is where we experience those feelings of anxiety and frustration. Through faith we can materialize our dreams.

An attitude of faith is accurate in situations where there seems to be no solution. Take a person with a certain illness, for example. If the person assumes that there is no cure and that it is all over, they begin to create in their mind a series of episodes of tragedy and pain. It won't be long before they start acting in the way their thoughts are directing them and their environment will perceive them in the same way, more so if they decide to believe that there is some chance to positively and optimistically face such a situation and assume that this will not be their end, and that on the contrary, unexpected things could happen in their life that will change everything in their favor, then very possibly a miracle will happen.

Faith is strengthened by habit. As a person experiences one benefit as a product of their faith, they feel more confident to achieve another. There is something important to clarify about faith and that is that it has two poles, one positive and one negative. Both are equally powerful. It takes the same quantity and quality of thoughts to make faith bring a result, whatever it is. Neither faith nor the mind recognizes what is positive or what is negative, they only respond to the attention and intensity that we give to each thought. Although we have talked about this before, it is relevant to bring it back here, because we know that thoughts lead us to act according to the nature of what we are thinking and those actions will definitely bring about similar consequences. Let's see then what kind of material we are using in the construction of our mental plane. Faith comes from a thought we can believe that something positive or negative will happen and according to the force we are giving that thought we are perceiving more and more real. This is how we gradually create in our mind what we will later experience on the material plane. We are creative gods with the power of our mind.

Think of a great project that already exists, something that you like, that perhaps has impacted you or you find it extraordinary, for example, airplanes, the spectacular constructions of Dubai, the media, the most sophisticated cars, even television and a lot of wonders that have been built throughout history. Now think of other types of projects or events that are less constructive or less beneficial, such as wars, weapons, suicides, murders, and so many other things that we could mention, which leave wounds on people and whole nations; all these, both those who work for good and those who do not, had the same beginning... **"one thought"**. A simple starting point, but at the same time great and powerful. All events began in the same way, they had the same source, but what was the source full of and what was the motivation?

The source (mind) in this case is like an empty vessel, each person fills it according to what they hear and what they see, with the information they frequent. The mind processes thoughts, words, images, sounds; it is a huge storage cellar. Everything, absolutely everything is stored there, even what we consider insignificant is perceived by it. It is a powerful recorder of everything that happens in the environment and then transforms it into memories and habits, which little by little will become the foundations of our life. This is the way we have learned to assume the circumstances, but this does not mean that there are no other ways of facing life, perhaps easier and that give us better results. Faith should become one of those primary foundations for every person. It is a thought of security, which in alliance with the mind gives us the right tools that will work in order to drive us in the achievement of our goals and dreams. It doesn't matter what kind of circumstance you are living through, whether it is an emotional, financial, or health difficulty or whether it is because everything is going well, but you would like to take your life to a higher level. Maybe improve your physical condition, improve the way you relate to people, be more prosperous, be more successful in business or any issue in any area of your life that you want to improve. All this is possible if you decide to sow the seed of faith in your mind and heart with the certainty that everything you long for and believe you can have; you will see it come true. You just have to keep in mind that your mind will put you in the place where you allow it to take you. It has, as I mentioned, its own tools that will empower that thought. I'd like to share a phrase, which has been immensely meaningful and inspiring to my husband and I, throughout our relationship: **"As far as our mind goes, that' s how far we'll go."** And we have experienced this, clearly and powerfully, on our life's journey.

Now ask yourself, what kind of thoughts am I harboring in my mind?

Remember that they will produce a result. Be very smart about focusing your attention. Put a filter on the information you let into your brain. Remember that the thoughts are in you, and you are not in your thoughts. Generate thought waves charged with truth, harmony, health and peace. Stop everything that leads you to waste your time. Stay close to everything that brings value to your life. Learn from people who know more than you do. Respect your fellow man. Give up your post. Listen carefully when someone speaks to you. Take care of nature. Read books that teach you how to manage your finances and help you grow as a person. Laugh more. Share more and better time with your family. Set a time limit on social networking. This doesn't mean to withdraw from the world, but to choose for you everything that will promote you to live a more peaceful, fluid and abundant life. Be an inspiration to others. How about starting by being an inspiration to your children, your family, and your surroundings?

Anything is possible. Everything is possible if you make the decision to be yourself, not to be someone who walks as if they have no free will (freedom to make their own conscious decisions). Anyone who manages to control their emotions has the power to maintain their mood in a constant state of serenity that allows them, even in the most difficult moment, to think with a cool head and make the wisest decision.

Recognize that the thoughts you harbor in your mind will be the foundation of your life and they will put you as high or as low as you can get. Decide today what kind of foundation you will continue with from here on out.

Success and happiness are within you. Strength and power flow from within you. Look within your thoughts for your qualities, your personal security, your potential, your beauty, your initiative, your faith, your vitality, your intelligence, and your ability to love yourself and others.

Do not give up the privilege of writing your life story to anyone. Take responsibility for your life, be strong, authentic, and simple. Provide a sincere friendship, accept yourself as you are and accept others as they are. Don't try to change anyone in your own way. Renew your habits. Dream a lot more. Feel free to sow good seeds wherever you go. Be excellent in everything you do. Put the stamp of excellence on all your work, not to be recognized or to be compared with anyone else, but for your own satisfaction. Forgive from love, understanding that if you forgive it is not because you are too good, but because we all deserve another chance. Free yourself from resentment because it ties your life to bitterness. Resentment sickens not only the soul, but the physical body as well. The body is the reflection of the soul.

You may think that there are too many things to improve, but from the bottom of my heart I want to tell you that it is worth committing ourselves to being better. They are not rules or impositions, they are open truths for anyone who wants to receive them. If you really want to be happy, do not hold on to the knowledge, experience it for yourself and you will receive your rewards in time. Rewards that will enlarge your life and the lives of those around you. Applied knowledge is wisdom and wisdom is acting wisely.

Now I ask myself if we really want to be happy or if what we really expect is to be made happy; this is when another question emerges: - What am I willing to do to find my happiness again?

Whatever your level of commitment is to find your happiness, that is the level at which you will discover that happiness is within you, in your mind; it is completely linked to your state of mind, to your decision and your commitment to be happy.

CHAPTER ELEVEN
"Happiness and Success"

As you may have noticed, the title of this chapter is headed by the word happiness and then by the word success; for that is the order in which I think they should remain in our lives, one as a result of the other. Thus understanding that it is not success that brings us happiness, but happiness that should lead us to experience success.

Success

I'd like to start with two questions: - The first: Do you know the meaning of the word success?

We usually link it to money, fame or recognition. Each person can give their definition according to their perception, but the concept I personally identify with is the following: The word success is derived from another word that means output or end result. That is, to experience success, we must first forge it.

When you begin to see success, not as something you need to feel in fullness, but as you learn to live happily with yourself and your environment, without falling into stagnation or conformity, you will be able to feel successful in every step you take. In each small goal that you set for yourself and that you manage to carry out. In the work that you do in your job, in your role as a father or mother, as a husband or wife, as a son or daughter. Being successful means that you feel personal satisfaction, about your own life and what you become every day. This satisfaction does not depend on external recognition, but on what you yourself know you have achieved. From your inner struggles won, overcoming your own fears. From your effort to be better and better and your desire to change, not only for your own well-being, but also for the people around you. To be successful is to feel grateful for the life you have, but with your sights set on higher challenges to achieve.

We often see people with a seemingly successful life fall into depression, drug or alcohol addiction and in some cases even suicide. This leads me to become more and more convinced of the importance of learning to be happy first, or rather learning to discover the happiness that is in fact already imprinted within each of us. It is essential to prepare ourselves for success when it comes, and in that way it is not a variable, but a constant in our daily lives. Not because we need it to be happy, but because without seeking it, it becomes a result of our daily life.

Success is not measured by the type of activity in which it is achieved, it is measured by the positive impact it generates in the life of the person who achieves it, focused on service to others.

Happiness

The second question is: What do you think is the meaning of happiness?

Perhaps you might think of it as enjoying financial security , physical beauty, travel, material goods, or getting married and having children, and so on. All these things have their own importance, but happiness does not lie within. . About this question, I also want to share with you my concept and that is that happiness is equal to tranquility, to love, to feel inner peace, to live with joy and passion. The rest has to come as an addition. Happiness is a path that we must travel every day, but not a destination to try to reach.

"A person is happy, when they find satisfaction in everything they do"

Happiness, a wonderful word that I love, whose meaning can be wide and each person will assume it in his own way, but I will summarize it *as a way of life*. It will result in an existence of joy, peace, abundance, wisdom and longevity.

Time

Hours pass quickly and sometimes we feel that time is not enough, especially when we do not know how to manage it well. You may have heard the phrase "time is money" and yet we often waste it on things that really don't add anything uplifting to our lives. Time is an immensely valuable gift, but what we do with it is in our own hands. The time that goes away is never recovered. Every second, literally as much as we would like, we cannot recover it; we only have the one that comes from here on and with that time we can do powerful things that will make our life grow and evolve. It is time to love and value time if we really want to experience a fuller and happier life.

I leave you with a question, for you to analyze and answer for yourself, according to the results you are experiencing in your life at this very moment: **What am I doing with my time?** Am I using it productively or am I letting it go as if it were worthless?

Winning Mind

We were all endowed with the same wealth of mind. Each person observes their life from their own perspective. If we look from the point of view of a winner, we always find in misfortunes or failures, a new reason to continue and move forward. That is the wonderful thing about learning to see defeat as a natural part of life; to see it as that moment that gives us the best opportunity to continue, to shake off the dust of the fall and to get back up with the encouragement and joy of knowing that we can try again and that we are given the opportunity to fail without judgment. A winner always identifies the obstacles, but prepares with strength and speed to jump them; and if for some reason he falls, he will surely get up again and continue, regardless of whether he wins that race or not. Reaching the finish line does not mean you have to be the first to arrive or that you have to pass over others. It means that everyone runs at their own pace and achieves their own successes; and success has nothing to do with external recognition, it's just about personal satisfaction (mentioned above). But such successes will not come unless you have prepared yourself to achieve them, as a result of a life of constant happiness, based on values and principles.

Decision

The life of human beings is made up of moments, all we experience daily are moments of calm or storm, but, in the end, it will always be our attitude that will define the result. The event may seem negative, but with a wise and calm attitude we can transform it into a constructive moment from which we learn something that gives us strength and motivation to continue, or on the contrary, if we react negatively to adverse situations, these could become even worse and this will generate as a result not only a bad moment, but a complete ruined day, both for me and for those around me. So if things don't turn out the way we want them to or the way we expect them to, we shouldn't leave the rest of the day to one moment.

Let's train our minds to assume everything can happen with an attitude of serenity, let's learn to feel confident that every situation always has a good purpose. Keeping calm produces better results. When there is calm and tranquility, better ideas emerge. A sweet word calms anger. A smile can give hope to a face dull with bitterness. If someone explodes in anger I don't have to react in the same way, because everyone gives according to what he or she has in their heart. If we learn to be in control of our mind and not to let it drift, guided by a belief system based on the information we brought with us, if we freely make the decision to maintain inner peace, life has to be more promising and the results we expect have to come. This is where we become free and autonomous.

Throughout our lives, we have been acting automatically, guided by the information with which the system constantly bombards us, but not by our own decision. We think we are deciding, but we really aren't. (Give yourself the opportunity to consciously observe and realize how the media manipulates minds)

We cannot expect a different outcome, speaking and acting lightly, without stopping to analyze the direction we have taken in our lives.

-I recommend watching the movie: *The Matrix*.

We all yearn to be happy in life, I don't think anyone wishes otherwise. So, start by renewing your thoughts and you can use all your senses to achieve this. It's about learning to master your mind and start changing your behaviors through new habits. Habits that open your mind to experience other types of sensations and experiences that you may not have known. May your day not only be about opening your eyes and waiting for night to come again, but may each sunrise be filled with motivation to do things that you had not risked doing before.

A very positive habit, which allows us to start the day with the best attitude, is to be grateful and to put all our activities in the hands of the Divine Source, whatever the spiritual belief that each one of us has. To raise a prayer to heaven each morning and give thanks for the privilege we have of being able to see, hear, walk and for the gift of being alive. To be grateful for every molecule in our wonderful body, to feel that gratitude for everything that makes it possible for us to wake up again every day.

You could continue to look at yourself in the mirror and not only see your reflection in it, but look beyond the physical body, see the special being that you are. Talking to you and expressing yourself is everything that makes you feel good, everything that enhances your self-esteem and empowers you. You will see that your body will magically react to the sound of your voice.

And how about starting your day not only thinking about yourself, but also giving a special and affectionate greeting to the people you live with. A "good morning" and a smile will be enough to generate a vibration of harmony in the place you are. This is a great way to get out of your house and start your day at work, which connects you to the field of all possibilities for extraordinary things to happen in your life and so does the work you do at home and that is where you will stay during the day.

What we declare with our language, is what we generate in the material. Getting up in a bad mood and leaving our house vibrating with that negative frequency, what it will do is trigger a series of events of the same category. It's normal for many people to say, "I got up on the wrong side of the bed today!" I want to tell you; they are already predicting to themselves that this day will definitely not be the best. I would like to clarify that I am not saying that we will never have difficult moments or days, those that even with all your good attitude, will not go very well, but that is where we must maintain firmness of character and a serene attitude, surely joy and calm will flourish preserving the structure of your state of peace.

Happiness means finding a state of harmony and tranquility even in those adverse moments. That same state of mind helps us to stay focused on our goals and thus allows us to enjoy a prosperous life in all areas.

Happiness is a free gift that belongs to all of us. Many times we get confused and look for it in things that really can't replace it. We usually believe it is in money, a person, a promotion, a car, a house or a trip, but we forget that where we have to look first is in the heart. Many people are unaware that within themselves they have the capacity and strength to face life's storms. Creativity comes out when there are pressures.

There are those who, feeling desperate about a financial crisis, about the loss of a loved one or about not having a job or about any complicated situation that we human beings sometimes go through, become so weak that they reach the point of losing their reason or take their own lives, just because they do not know that there were not only one but several solutions to their problem.

We need to constantly and consciously nourish our brain with healthy information, so that when we have to take on a challenge, we do so with integrity. We must free ourselves from that mentality, that in the face of an adverse situation what we do is feel vulnerable and fragile. Usually, when faced with a difficulty, we look for ways to excuse ourselves or to feel victimized, but this does not really help at all; what empowers us and catapults us forward is to take responsibility for our affairs with courage and bravery, facing challenges as our own. Hiding our heads in the sand and waiting for things to change on their own will not solve anything. It is worth taking as an example of life the attitude that the eagles assume when the storm approaches, they rise to the heights above the storm; so we when we find ourselves going through some storm, we must raise our thoughts above them.

Let us remember that we are creators and that we have the power to generate what we want to see manifested in our reality.

Dream

We usually say that dreaming does not cost anything and in correspondence to this, the range of all possibilities surprises us with wonderful gifts. If we dream we provoke the Universe to conspire in favor of our dreams. Dreams allow us to travel to wonderful places and take us where we never imagined we could go. They fill our lives with motivation. For that reason when we dream let's do it with faith, because faith is that confidence that something that at the moment is not tangible, will surely come. Whoever dreams has the privilege of being surprised by life, because when you see something come true that was born in your mind, you definitely feel pleased and you will surely want to dream again and this time with something bigger. Perhaps among your dreams is a trip to some beautiful place, establish a company, a job promotion or something else, but as simple or complex as it may seem, just keep it in your mind, with your unwavering faith that you will get it and this will surely come. You will begin to find on the road everything that that dream will bring you closer. You'll find the right people in the right places, the perfect times and everything you need to see your dreams come true. You will see how perfect timing will align everything in your favor and your dreams will blossom.

To be like children

I feel in a special way that this book is for everyone who dares to have an innocent mind like the one children have, because they have a wonderful perception of life. They believe that they can do everything and that they can have everything. Children enjoy every day, they are confident. They may get upset and cry, but within minutes they are laughing and playing again. They have the virtue of dreaming no matter how absurd it seems. There are so many beautiful things that we adults should learn from them; we would regain our pure essence. That which allows us to be free from sorrow and fear. That transparent essence of being as we really are, no matter what others think. To be ourselves and to enjoy every second of our life to the fullest with the strength and vitality that we used to do as children.

We are all born with that clean essence, but the environment contaminates and changes much of it. Now that we are aware of this, we have the opportunity to recover everything that belongs to us in its own right and the best thing of all is that we have it within us.

Believe

To have the conviction that happiness flows from my inner being and to be happy I just have to make the decision to be happy, because even with all the difficult situations we have to go through, we always have a lot of new opportunities to be happy. We have all the tools that connect us to that inner happiness. We have the gift of life; we have a powerful brain which is a great richness that we human beings have. All we need to emerge to an extraordinary life is to think that we can do it. I can assure you that these are not just words, but evidenced truths that you cannot lose the privilege of proving with your own life experience, that they really are. It doesn't matter if some in your family have died from a hereditary disease, you will be the exception because everything is a result of information. It doesn't matter if everyone in your family has been poor, decide that you won't be and cut the ties of scarcity. Decide today that from you will begin to emerge wonderful changes that will reach all your relatives and nearby environment. Begin by knowing your potential and believe that you have everything to be happy and you will be.

Sow

There is a universal law that says that everything you sow has a harvest and the harvest is always much more than what you sow. Whether you sow for good or not, you reap more than you sow. Based on this law, I want to tell you with certainty that when you decide to sow happiness in others, you reap abundantly more happiness. One of the greatest satisfactions a person can experience in life is to make someone else happy. You can practice it; you will see what it feels like. When we make someone happy, there will be other people waiting to make us happy.

There are many ways to bring happiness, for example with a smile, a word of encouragement, a call, a hug, a gift of a good piece of clothing, being a support in a difficult moment, shaking someone's hand, offering sincere congratulations, an "I love you" never hurt anyone, a word of gratitude, being a messenger of good news and solutions, being a peacemaker, being a generator of joy. And I know that everyone can add new and different ways to sow happiness in their daily lives. Use your creativity and be guided by your essence.

Be decisive

No one can excuse themselves in poverty, illness, disability, unemployment, frustration, a vice or any other circumstance that they are going through at the moment in order not to get ahead. He is just living in his comfort zone. If you want proof of that, look at the number of people who have managed to do so despite their circumstances. Many people after a serious illness have healed themselves. Others, after losing a member of their body, have gone on to do even greater things than they did when they had their whole body. There are those who were born without an organ in their body and still live like any other person who has all their organs. There are many businessmen who have gone bankrupt and have risen again and even stronger. Others were orphaned since childhood, but fought and today are what they dreamed of being and have what they dreamed of having. I invite you to investigate and read for yourself, lots of biographies of people who have become true heroes of their own lives and who today are great examples of personal growth, simply because they have been decisive in their decision not to let themselves be defeated by any circumstance and they found within themselves everything they needed to achieve their goals.

Happiness motivates us to set goals, to dream and to project ourselves. To be happy is a challenge, it is a prize that is within everyone's reach, but only the brave ones have access to it.

The sky, as many believe, is not above the clouds; the sky is here on earth, in your mind and in your heart. Heaven is a state of the soul. It is the connection to ourselves and to the Divine Source. It is a path, not a destination to be reached. Heaven is a state of peace and tranquility. It is happiness, and happiness comes from transforming your mindset.

Tell me how you think and I'll tell you who you are, because the way you think, you talk, you act; that's what your life becomes.

If for an instant you think you are not capable of achieving happiness, if you feel you cannot resolve some adverse circumstance you are going through, I invite you to connect with the Source, with the Universal Mind, God or whatever you prefer to call it and it will fill you with its light. That Divine Source is within each of us and in everything; we just have to be more sensitive and try to quiet the mental noise that continually keeps us distracted.

"Today my mind will be more attentive and my heart will be receptive" - Joel Osteen

Anything you want to be, you can be. Anything you want to do you can do. Your dreams, goals and projects, you can see them come true. The greatest power is in your mind. If you can put it in your mind, you can make it happen. Work on your personal growth, read good books that open your mind to different and better ways of life. Make your moments of solitude, great moments to grow and even improve your way of living and relating to others. Respect the ideas and thoughts of each person. Be yourself, do not lose your essence and if you lost it at some point, recover it, you're still on time. Live intensely. Eat healthy. Exercise your body. Relax your mind. Meditate in silence. Be early for your appointments. Honor your word. Keep your promises. Smile a lot. Embrace more. Brighten up the lives of those around you. Think big. Love your family and accept them as they are. Do something you are passionate about. Try to do what you love, even if it is only for a short time, but don't stop.

This is the time to start again. . Life is full of opportunities, don't let them pass you by. Trust yourself more. Talk less and listen more. Even in the wisdom of Solomon's proverbs, this theme is alluded to when he says, ***"Within the multitude of words, folly is not lacking"*** Proverbs 10-19

Let's take the time to write down dreams and goals on paper, for it's a way of letting the Universe know that these are special thoughts and that we long for them to come true.

Happiness is the mirror in which the state of our soul is reflected. The fuller we feel inside, the happier we are. We all enjoy possessing material things, but they are not the ones that bring true happiness. They only provide us with moments of emotional ups and downs, only passing moments.

Absolutely everything we experience every day has to do with the state of our inner being. With that capacity to assume each circumstance with courage and wisdom, with strength, joy, love; above all with the certainty of knowing that there is a powerful force acting on our behalf, providing us with all the necessary tools to be truly happy from within.

Advice for life

I want to motivate you from the depths of my heart to discover that valuable treasure you have inside you. The one that will allow you to fly as high as you wish and that will drive you to achieve your dreams. I challenge you to be happy and the time to take on this challenge is now, don't put off until tomorrow what you can start doing today and you will soon see how everything that you thought was impossible to achieve becomes a reality; perhaps because of your age, because you don't have money, because you don't have time, because you don't belong to a certain social class, because you are this or that way or simply because your mind was out of focus.

The day to be happy is today. This is the time to take that step of faith in yourself and launch into life without fear, without looking at the past however it may have been. It is time to discover your inner power.

Start by practicing what you have learned in this book. It is dedicated especially to you, with the certainty that if you decide to renew your mindset, you will begin to experience positive changes leading to a fuller life.

Be happy even if things are not the color or shape you expect. It is a decision you must make now, remember that things are seen according to the perception of your mind, gray is also a beautiful color and just because the day is this color, it does not mean that your mood should be down, or that if the sky is bright blue, your heart should be happy.

Let go of those old disempowering behavior patterns, make decisions that impact your life in a different way. Adopt new habits. Habits shape your destiny.

Learn from mistakes without judging yourself or anyone else. Don't blame others for what you haven't accomplished. Do not put your happiness in anyone's hands, take it as a challenge and do not stop until you reach it, surely you can do it.

Don't wait until you feel that everything is perfect to start being happy, because then you will never be. Life sometimes brings situations that we don't expect and surprises us with unexpected pain or loss, but it is all part of life. You know that sometimes you love someone and that someone does not love you, sometimes you do not have a job, you don't have money in your pocket or maybe you lose a loved one. There are times when those we think are our friends fail us or someone offends us. Sometimes children are rebellious, the body gets sick, we don't find the right way to reach our goals, the life projects are not clear or we don't have a partner; and we could continue to list a number of reasons for not being happy and get immersed in victimizing, but inside each one of us there is an endless number of strengths and virtues waiting to be used as a springboard to happiness; We only have to undertake this journey inside ourselves, to discover that we are endowed with powers we do not even imagine are there, with which our goals are transformed into realities and our ordinary life into an extraordinary and happy life!!!.

Sometimes adversity plays an important role in bringing out the full potential of the human mind. Many people have turned their lives upside down by finding no other option but to throw themselves into the void of uncertainty, face difficult circumstances and test all their creativity. They decide to redirect their lives, making wise choices, driven by their inner strength.

Many through their hard experiences, become great motivators, for there is nothing that prevents a being from rising from his worst fall. Enough of complaining, of feeling defeated and sad. Enough of excuses and of wasting time in the same thoughts about everything that needs to be done to change our lives. Enough of feeling offended by small things. Let us be aware that time advances and waits for no one, if you decide to stay maybe nothing will happen, but if you decide to get up and go out and enjoy life, you will be able to experience new and wonderful experiences that one by one will form the pages of your own history.

It is never too late to discover your talents, to start a professional career, to learn to play a musical instrument that you like or to practice your favorite sport, to write a book, to get married, to have children, to start a career or to have your own company. You probably have hidden talents that you don't know about yet, but they remain within you, waiting to be discovered.

Let go of all the unnecessary burdens you carry. . Let go of all those thoughts of pain, sickness and old age. Remove from your lexicon the cliché that with age come all ailments. This is only in the mind and you create it when you speak it. Keep in mind that words are not swept away by the wind, they create and generate results.

Free yourself from grudges, for they do make the body of the unforgiving sick at heart. I make a parenthesis to remind you that no one hurts us, we ourselves are the ones who create and harbor that feeling. In ourselves is the decision to allow those words or negative attitudes of others to enter our lives and hurt us, or we put a stop and do not allow them to enter our hearts. If we truly desire to enjoy a long and full life, we must learn to forgive from love and not because we feel that there is an evil being who has hurt us who must be forgiven.

Words powerfully create your future. If negative thoughts come to you about yourself, some situation or person, watch your words about it because you will be creating more of the same.

Be careful how you express thoughts about yourself and your life. These statements become your reality. This present you live in today is a result of the seeds you sowed yesterday.

If only we could understand that there is an invisible power willing to help us and that it acts on our behalf, all that is needed is to make the decision to reinvent our thoughts. We only need faith to believe that we can make our life not just ordinary, but extraordinary. Hell and heaven are within each of us, not specific places. They are states of the soul and only each one decides in which of the two it wants to live. We give life to one or the other.

Let us master our emotions and not let them master us. Let us take the reins of our life with love and good attitude, that is our responsibility. Let us cultivate the garden of our thoughts.

Let's carefully observe the environment in which we move and start today to renew our daily habits. These are small changes that will cause important and valuable results. Let's encourage those habits that are linked to joy, health, peace and love.

It is worth mentioning that there is no material good that can make a human being completely happy, as much as inner peace. That is why you should face your fears and focus on your goals, we already know that the only way to overcome fears is by facing them; in the end we will see that they were only an illusion. If we succeed, let us enjoy the triumph, but if we fail, let us remember that failures are powerful attempts to want to progress and live better, they are a learning experience, they remind us of the value of humility and stimulate our creativity.

It is not the circumstances that place people in a certain situation, it is their thoughts about that situation and their decisions about how they assume and face it, that make the difference. There are always one or more ways to get out of it and move on.

You can be the maker of a prosperous and happy destiny not only for yourself, but for your family and society.

We can be the pioneers of a society with principles and human values.Keep the family together. Respect the spaces and thoughts of others. Express ourselves well, our family, our friends and the place where we live. Offer help to those who need it. Be more caring. Value virtues more than material goods. Express love for people. Be more forgiving. Be honest. Always tell the truth. Let's free ourselves from remorse. Let go of arguments, it's better to be happy than to pretend to be right. Be grateful. Love and care for nature and animals.

It's these kinds of attitudes that definitely focus us on the right path to happiness, but the only way you'll know if the claim in this book is true is if you decide to put it into practice. You have in your hands the power to change your life in your own way. You have the guidelines to begin to somehow transform your family's history. You can be the one who sows the seed to see in them new forms of coexistence and harmony. Each person has the power to decide. Free will is a power that was given to us by the Universe, to make decisions freely. In other words, what determines the quality of our life is absolutely the decisions we make in each circumstance it presents to us.

Happiness depends on you. You decide when you want to start being happy and you are bound to reach the top of your dreams.

The magic is me!

Everything is possible for those who believe. Life is beautiful for those who, from their mind, want to see it that way. We do not have to be satisfied with living an ordinary life, when we can create an extraordinary life.

I have the magic within me. I can create the sun on a cloudy day. I can see the beauty in people's hearts, I can draw a rainbow with the colors of my life, I can reinvent myself in a thousand different ways every morning. I can talk by looking into the eyes. I can embrace because I know we are all one. I can say I love you without fear of not being accepted. I can understand that people make mistakes and decide not to judge them. I can be grateful. I can love unconditionally. I can dream unstoppably. I can be the eagle that roams the skies. I can stand my ground over time. I can achieve everything I set out to do. I can renew my habits. I can inspire joy and happiness. I can make people laugh. I can keep my balance in both successes and failures. I can elevate my mind to infinity. I can be compassion, commitment and loyalty. I can be will. I can simply be me. I can look to the future. I can simply, here and now, decide to be happy.

Affirmations that will help you cultivate new habits and that every time you declare them, will become a reality in your life. Positive affirmations empower us and connect us with our divine essence...

I AM PURE AND PERFECT LOVE. I AM PROSPEROUS. I AM HARMONIOUS. I AM ATTRACTIVE. I AM A PEACEMAKER. I AM JOY. I AM INFINITE INTELLIGENCE. I AM LOVING. I AM FUN. I AM YOUNG. I AM

POSITIVE. I AM BLESSED. I AM UNLIMITED ABUN-
DANCE. I AM A MAGNET FOR WEALTH. I ATTRACT
GOOD RELATIONSHIPS. I AM A BALANCED PERSON.
I AM A CALM PERSON. I AM POWERFUL. I AM AB-
SOLUTE HARMONY. I AM ADMIRABLE BEAUTY. I AM
INSPIRATION TO THE WORLD.

I AM STRENGTH. I AM VITALITY. I AM SUC-
CESSFUL IN ALL THAT I UNDERTAKE. I HAVE EV-
ERYTHING I NEED TO BE HAPPY. I AM PERFECT
HEALTH. I AM BRAVE. I AM CAPABLE. I TRUST IN
MYSELF. I AM COMFORTABLE WITH MY BODY. I AM
A SPECIAL PERSON. MY EMOTIONS ARE IN PERFECT
BALANCE. I APPROVE OF MYSELF. I FOCUS ON MY
GOALS AND ACHIEVE THEM. I AM GENEROUS. I
LET MY INNER LIGHT SHINE. I CONTROL MY EMO-
TIONS. I FEEL GOOD. I AM GRATEFUL. MY SELF-ES-
TEEM IS HIGH. I ACCEPT MYSELF WITH MY FAULTS
AND WEAKNESSES. I AM A UNIQUE BEING. I AM ALL
HAPPINESS.

*"Every man is capable of transforming his life with
thought"*

Some of the highlighted phrases were taken from the following books:

-The Bible- Reina Valera

-Think and grow rich -Napoleon Hill

-The monk who sold his Ferrari -Robin Sharma

-The seven spiritual laws of success: Deepak Chopra

-A course in miracles

-The power of intention: Wayne Dyer

- One minute millonaire - Mark Victor Hansen

- Man's search for meaning- Viktor Frankl

Made in United States
North Haven, CT
17 April 2022

18233634R00093